PREACHING AND ETHICS

Preaching and Its Partners
A series edited by Paul Scott Wilson

PREACHING AND PRACTICAL MINISTRY
Ronald J. Allen

PREACHING AND WORSHIP
Thomas H. Troeger

PREACHING AND ETHICS
Arthur Van Seters

PREACHING AND HOMILETICAL THEORY
Paul Scott Wilson

PREACHING AND ETHICS

Arthur Van Seters

© Copyright 2004 Arthur Van Seters

All rights reserved. For permission to reuse content, please contact Copyright Clearance Center, 222 Rosewood Drive, Danvers, MA 01923, (978) 750-8400, www.copyright.com.

Biblical quotations, unless otherwise noted, are from the *New Revised Standard Version Bible*, copyright 1989, Division of Christian Education of the National Council of the Churches of Christ in the United States of America. Used by permission. All rights reserved.

Bible quotations marked J.B. Phillips are reprinted by permission of Simon & Schuster, from *The New Testament in Modern English*, revised edition, translated by J. B. Phillips. © 1958, 1960, 1972 by J. B. Phillips.

Sermon in the appendix was written for Proper 24, October 17, 2004 entry in *Preaching Word and Witness* (New Berlin, Wisc.: Liturgical Publications). Printed here by permission of Liturgical Publications. All rights reserved.

Cover design: Michael A. Domínguez
Cover art: © 1998 Artville
Interior design: Wynn Younker/Elizabeth Wright
Art direction: Michael A. Domínguez

This book is printed on acid-free, recycled paper.

Visit Chalice Press on the World Wide Web at
www.chalicepress.com

10 9 8 7 6 5 4 3 2 1   04 05 06 07 08 09

Library of Congress Cataloging-in-Publication Data

Van Seters, Arthur, 1934-
  Preaching and ethics / Arthur Van Seters.
    p. cm.
  ISBN 0-8272-2976-3 (pbk. : alk. paper)
  1. Preaching. 2. Christian ethics. I. Title.
BV4235.E75V36 2004
251–dc22

2004008676

Printed in the United States of America

To
our five sons,
David, Stephen, Tim, Philip, and Tom,
whose international vision
and
commitment to ethical responsibility
inspire hope

[handwritten: Atinsky quote]

[handwritten: we are the persecutors
not the persecuted
empire]

Contents

Preface	viii
1. Preaching Ethics	1
Introducing the Questions and a Model for Ethical Reflection	
2. Faith	21
Preaching a Gospel Perspective	
3. Moral Character	43
Preaching Christian Discipleship	
4. Norms	61
Preaching That Clarifies Gospel Requirements	
5. Situation and Context	79
Preaching That Engages Particularity	
6. Authority	99
To What Do Preachers Appeal?	
7. Preacher, Sermon, and Congregation	119
Preacher as Proclaimer of Ethics, Sermon as Ethical Communication, and Congregation as Ethical Community	
Appendix: An Ethical Sermon Illustrated	135
Notes	141
Author Index	161
Scripture Index	167
Subject Index	171

Preface

Preaching and ethics are so intimately connected it is surprising that very little has been published explicitly in this area until the last decade or so. Much attention has been focused on what we believe (theology) and ethics, and on the Bible and ethics. Similarly, in the field of homiletics both scripture and theology figure prominently. Why, then, has the implicit relationship between ethics and preaching not been more fully explicated? Perhaps the pejorative, "Don't preach at me!" which implies a certain negative moralizing, has made preachers and their teachers wary. But Jesus, who is at the center of Christian ethics, had no hesitation about preaching. Through his preaching he began to shape an ethical community of followers. Ethics, as homiletics professor Charles Campbell rightly argues, is implicit in the very act of preaching. As congregations gather for worship, many come hoping for ethical guidance rooted in Christian faith. They want to discern their way as a believing community in a changing world that is raising complex and difficult questions.

In the mid 1970s I was part of a small group that had the privilege of spending a week with lawyer and lay theologian William Stringfellow. On behalf of the staff of the Montreal Institute for Ministry, and on very short notice, I phoned him on Block Island to ask him to conduct a seminar. He surprised us with an immediate, affirmative response. In fact, he kept on surprising us as he engaged us that week in exploring political realities as profound moral issues through a most diligent reading of Romans 13 and Revelation 13. He helped us face our fallen human condition through the lens of an alternative vision in a gospel of Christian hope. In some way that encounter has been part of my journey to engage the subject of preaching and ethics. That journey has taken me several years as I have worked on the present project and interacted with the incisive thinking of Stringfellow, Walter Wink, Miroslav Volf, Walter Brueggemann, Barbara Brown Taylor, Ron Allen, and Charles Campbell (among others).

When Chalice Press approached me several years ago to write the present volume, I was taken aback. I had taught preaching for more than twenty-five years and had done research in the area of societal dimensions of preaching, but relating preaching and ethics as a whole was something quite new. So I did what homileticians often do: I turned to a former colleague (from my years at the Vancouver School of Theology) in the person of ethicist Terry Anderson. With both his enthusiastic encouragement and rigorous challenges, I have found this an exciting adventure–though still very much a work in progress. I make no apology, therefore, for structuring my approach to ethical reflection on Anderson's *Walking the Way: Christian Ethics as a Guide*.[1] I have re-ordered his "base points" and take responsibility for how I have used his material. I have also augmented his work with numerous other readings that reflect a wide range of ethical perspectives in order to explore specifically and systematically the role of preaching in relation to ethics as a discipline.

As I began research for this volume with the hope that it would also be concrete and practical, I descended into a period of mass confusion. How would I sort through endless issues, articles, and experiences that came more quickly to my awareness than my organizational systems could handle? I had to develop ways to organize, catalogue, and sort through massive amounts of material without becoming overwhelmed. I started to clip at least several newspaper items a day and to sort them under broad headings (economics, environment, biotechnology, health care, poverty, sexuality, capital punishment, war, etc.) and built a set of shelves with these labels. I developed computer folders for issues (by subject), a media file, sermon references, a bibliography, biblical texts, theological themes, stories, and so forth. This allowed me to file an item without having to decide on its use until sometime later. Sermon preparation is not just around next Sunday's sermon. Making notes along the way and having a system for keeping track can save time in the long run.

Because this study is intended primarily as a text for preachers, congregations, and seminary students, I offered a series of midweek studies in my home congregation of Armour Heights Presbyterian Church in Toronto. These were followed by sermons on the themes explored. I am indebted to this group and the congregation as they wrestled with difficult moral issues (genetics, legalized gambling, poverty, and physician-assisted mercy-killing). Their faith, questions, arguments, and encouragement left a lasting impression on me and on this volume. This experience was extended further following my first draft of this book when I gave another series of workshops at St. Andrew's Presbyterian Church, also in Toronto.

The acid test of any work, particularly one on ethics, is what happens when a nation and, indeed, the world are confronted by a totally new reality. The events of September 11, 2001, challenged preachers at the very core of their homiletics–a challenge filled with ethical dilemmas. On September 12 I began teaching a class at the Toronto School of Theology. Together we explored much of this text in the light of that event as well as the usual kinds of things students seek to question, discover, and extend. The model offered here helped us to both probe ethical dimensions of this new experience and ponder how to preach in light of our reflections. One student (from the U.S.) gave a moving sermon on the issue of patriotism. Currently, I am leading a doctoral seminar that has probed the present volume even further and effected significant changes. I thank these homiletics colleagues for my continuing learning.

I also wish to thank several readers who worked through all or much of previous drafts: Rev. Bill Middleton and elder Michael Nettleton (both from Armour Heights Church), homileticians Stephen Farris and John Rottman, and ethicists Terry Anderson and the late Roger Hutchinson. Most of all, I have been fortunate to have had Paul Scott Wilson as the editor of this series and an untiring source of general guidance, constructive criticism, and thoughtful affirmation. Most recently, newly appointed Senior Editor of Chalice Press, Trent Butler, has given me gracious and incisive feedback that has energized me to work through this final draft in a spirit of hopefulness. I am indebted for the way these persons have suggested deletions, called for clarifications and additions, and contributed immeasurably to my progress–though I am entirely responsible for what I chose to modify or change. Finally, to my wife, Rowena, I am grateful for infinite patience, a sharp eye in reading and rereading every draft, and a source of ethical inspiration. This latter contribution extends also to our five sons who have sought to live their ethics with uncommon commitment and have challenged me in mine. To them I happily dedicate this volume.

To the reader I add this note. Because I have described this as a work in progress, I hope that it will be read with a critical eye (including my fairly extensive endnotes!) and that readers, bringing their own perspectives and insights, will move its arguments forward and add their own examples. While I have offered some ways to implement my proposals homiletically, I respect the inventiveness of preachers in wrestling with the best way to live out these ideas in their own settings. In the end, I trust that all will be inspired to live their faith and proclaim it by word and action ultimately as servants of Christ, the incarnate Word.

Arthur Van Seters
Toronto

1

PREACHING ETHICS

Introducing the Questions and a Model for Ethical Reflection

A congregation found itself deeply divided. The divisive moral issue involved providing sanctuary for desperate refugee claimants. Naturally, they turned to an ethicist for help. No neophyte, she had often been invited to mediate in an ethical debate. But this experience surprised her. Usually, opposing sides are so committed to the rightness of their own viewpoint that just grasping what each side really means or uncovering the underlying value assumptions makes the task complicated and tedious. Often the best that can be hoped for is agreeing to disagree. But this particular congregation had been nurtured, challenged, and inspired by years of preaching. This gave them a common language, an openness to be surprised by scripture, a growing understanding of what it means to be a community of baptized people, and a sense of respect for others as persons created by God. The ethicist noted the difference that preaching can make in enabling the church to live out its discipleship in faithfulness to Jesus Christ, that is, to be a moral community and engage puzzling ethical dilemmas when they emerge.

This book seeks to explore the relationship between preaching and ethics to help congregations live out the gospel. It is not a primer in Christian ethics. Nor is it assumed that the goal of preaching is to develop ethicists as such. Rather, our purpose is to *enable preachers to contribute to the ethical formation and behavior* of a people who see themselves as a community of Christians and who seek to discern what this means.

Preaching can make a difference in enabling discipleship.

This book adopts a particular approach to ethics, which this opening chapter will introduce. Similarly, this chapter will make certain homiletical assumptions explicit. But first we must face questions and issues that confront preachers, congregations, and, indeed, the larger communities within which the church gathers to worship and discover its way as God's people.

Facing Difficult Questions

For preacher and for congregation, engaging ethics is not merely an intellectual exercise. Persistent, often puzzling, sometimes painful questions confront each of us. Some arise from the world around us; others come from scripture; and some from the long history of the church. While the listening congregation may already be aware of some of these, others may surprise them. In addition, ethics from a *Christian* perspective needs to grapple with the issue of secularity.

Questions from Culture

The word *culture* is an elastic term. It may refer to language, habits, ideas, and customs that enable us to communicate with one another, or it can refer to particular traditions that shape us, such as a West Indian culture or a Southern Baptist culture. Others use the term in speaking of a literary figure, such as T. S. Eliot, or of music, such as American jazz. Or we may have in mind the culture of pluralism in modern societies in which no voice or tradition has the shaping power of ancient Hellenism, or of the Catholic Church of the Middle Ages. In an age of mass communication, culture surrounds us, often enveloping us with subtle and suggestive influences or puzzling questions that become ethical debates. These frequently begin as news reports of some social development or scientific discovery.

Culture surrounds us, often enveloping us with subtle and suggestive influences or puzzling questions.

In March 1997, a news item described how the Roslin Institute near Edinburgh had successfully cloned a Dorset Finn sheep. From a single mammary gland of an adult sheep a research team of scientists had produced an entirely identical animal that they called Dolly. What the world's leading scientists said couldn't be done had become reality. "Now the question on everyone's mind was obvious. If they can clone sheep today, can they clone humans tomorrow?"[1]

The human genome project to map the genes in the human body has been largely completed. This roadmap has been named "The Book of Life" for all humankind, phrasing drawn from sacred scripture.[2] But will the sacredness of life be respected in the process? The preacher is sent back to the early chapters of Genesis to reflect further on our creation as creatures in God's image.

Even as we ponder our created connectedness with God, another news item appears. Jeremy Rifkin notes that the British patent office has granted patents to the Roslin Institute on its cloning process. This patent includes intellectual property rights over all patented inventions including those of human embryos. For the first time a national government is prepared to view a human being created through the process of cloning as an invention.[3]

Further ethical questions emerge. Will economics control the creation of human life? Embryonic human life, it seems, can be subjected to the power of life-science companies. Is this a new form of slavery, one reaching far beyond the racial slavery defeated in the U.S. Civil War more than a century ago? Will our children, learning about all of this, be able to distinguish between human life and inanimate objects? Are we now being regarded as "simple utilities to be bartered like so many commodities in the commercial arena?" At this point the columnist could not resist asking the God-question: "And, if cloned human embryos are in fact considered to be human inventions, then what becomes of our notion of God, the creator?"[4]

Does the preacher deal with these kinds of questions in a sermon? If so, how may it be done most helpfully? If the congregation has been following this discussion in the media, what, if anything, do they expect from a sermon that seeks to engage this subject? If reference is made to the genome project only in passing, might listeners wonder why it is not deemed important? When the preacher does decide to tackle it, some listeners may have little or no acquaintance with the topic. How does the preacher proceed? To what does the preacher appeal?

This issue of cloning is one among a myriad. Some are prominent in the media, such as the astronomical increase in legalized gambling or the military intervention of one country by another to save people from possible genocide. Sexual morality, abortion, gun control, prayer in public schools, global warming, persistent and soul-destroying poverty, domestic violence, euthanasia, and capital punishment may be added, and on and on.[5] A whole host of additional questions arise from the terrorist attacks on September 11. Why would suicide bombers do this? How should the United States and the world respond?[6] Another host of issues emerge from the astronomical incomes for CEOs and from their practice of exercising stock options just before their companies collapse.[7]

The proliferation of ethical conundrums easily overwhelms us to the point of numbness. How does one choose? When certain selections are made, who has the time, expertise, or courage to include them with some depth in preaching? The question is more poignant in a culture such as ours that seems to have a limited capacity for clear moral deliberation. In his seminal analysis of the state of ethics in Western society, Alasdair MacIntyre declares that the "most striking feature of contemporary moral utterance is that so much of it is used to express disagreements" in unending debates. "There seems to be no rational way of securing moral agreement in our culture."[8]

> *The "most striking feature of contemporary moral utterance is that so much of it is used to express disagreements" in unending debates.*

As questions emerge from our newspapers (or radios, TVs, novels, movies, the Internet, etc.), preachers turn to their Bibles and seek to prepare next Sunday's sermon. Similarly, congregations are often hoping that preachers will not duck moral questions but will offer faithful guidance. How are preachers to invite God's people to take the way of discipleship, to live more consistently with what they claim to believe?

Questions from Scripture

Preachers often appeal to the biblical prophets, the teaching of Jesus, and the correspondence of the apostles when they refer to ethical issues in their sermons.[9] Whatever may be implied in such appeals, they cannot ignore the fact that the interpretation of scripture is itself a controversial topic today.

The psalmist speaks personally and confessionally, "Your word is a lamp to my feet / and a light to my path" (Ps. 119:105). But how does a passage such as Genesis 47:13–26, describing the economic policy of Joseph in Egypt (which had the effect of enslaving not only all Egyptians but the Hebrew people as well), shed light?[10] Do we preach *against* the text in such a case? Is this a question of confusing narrative with law? How does each different genre contribute to our ethical perspective?[11] Other texts, such as regulations regarding the Sabbath year (Deut. 15), propose economic rearrangements that appear to stand over against our market-oriented society. These may sound strange to modern listeners. How do we preach on something such as comments of Jesus on divorce (Mt. 5:31–32) that seem so different from contemporary society's views?

How do we sort out which passages will have what kind of weight? Sometimes the text implies revelation, as when the prophets use the expression "Thus says the LORD." Elsewhere we find appeals to reason, as in Paul's Areopagus address (Acts 17:22–31). The chosenness of Israel is affirmed in Amos 3:2. But books such as Ruth and Jonah stress a broader perspective. Much of the New Testament (see especially Rom. 9–11) struggles with the same tension between the particularity of one people and the universal scope of the gospel. Many modern Bible students seek to differentiate between law in the Old Testament and grace in the New; but grace is seen in God's selection of Israel in Deuteronomy 7:7–9, and James 2:14–17 argues that "faith by itself, if it has no works, is dead."[12]

> *We are more responsible in our preaching if we acknowledge that scripture is a library, a diverse collection of voices, which cannot be easily synthesized to fit some modern notion of uniformity or consistency.*[13]

While scholars offer various explanations to resolve these tensions, this tautness in the text cautions us against any facile appeals to scripture. Indeed, Philip Wogaman reminds us that such tensions have persisted through two millennia of the church's history and remain unresolved.[14] But preachers should also note that scripture is often quite clear about what God requires of us (as we will see specifically when we turn to the Ten Commandments and the Sermon on the Mount in chap. 4). It asks questions of us and of our culture that can be challenging: How do we honor God in a secular, pluralistic culture? How do we show forgiveness of enemies? How do we transcend the covetousness built into a consumer society?

> *Preachers should not be afraid to raise these sorts of questions in their sermons.*

Questions from Church History

Many of our ethical questions are not new. The way in which the church has wrestled with ethics over the last two millennia can be of continuing validity. Here, we offer highly selective references drawing appreciatively on Philip Wogaman's extensive history of Christian ethics.[15]

In the opening centuries of its life the Christian church found itself in conflict with Roman society on such matters as wealth and poverty, sexuality, status and role, violence, and the political order. Origen emphasized God's law of nature over all human laws, while Tertullian used Christian standards to attack moral decline. Ignatius of Antioch argued that "the greatness of Christianity lies in its being hated by the world, not in its being convincing to it."[16] By the fourth century, when Christianity gained its freedom (and also political and cultural power), a new question arose: "How can one be sure who is really committed to the way of Christ rather than just expediently so?" Today, as the church returns to minority status, we are reminded that being on the margins may clarify our witness and sharpen our ethical distinctiveness.

> *Augustine articulated a vision of faith that lasted for a thousand years.*

As Rome fell, how could the church discern a new way? Augustine articulated an alternative vision of society that included a whole social ethic. The church is a wayfaring community (*in* but not altogether *of* the world) that lives by grace. Today we sometimes get discouraged about the impact of Christian ethics on the world around us. Charles Cochrane said, Augustine moved beyond the reigning cultural rationality of his day to articulate a vision of faith seeking understanding that lasted for a thousand years.[17]

When the church loses its way, what then? In the Reformation, the positive pull of theology challenged both the church within and the world outside. The Reformers of the sixteenth century struggled with this question with particular reference to the relationship between the church and the state. Martin Luther insisted that the kingdom of God cannot be brought about through the kingdom of the world. John Calvin emphasized the sovereignty of God over all spheres of life, calling Christians to be responsive to God in each of them. The ethic of the Anabaptists, however, was not in the public realm, but stressed internal discipline within their alternative communities of faith.

In the seventeenth to nineteenth centuries, the increasing influence of science and reason (versus revelation) broke with the Augustinian notion of faith seeking understanding. Ethical thought focused on the *individual's* freedom to choose good or evil. Human beings are fundamentally independent. They form societies through contractual agreements that protect a natural right to life, liberty, and property. These centuries centered thought on human rights, all without much reference to God.[18] In this setting Joseph Butler sought to demonstrate the reasonableness of Christianity. He argued that revelation lends fresh authority to natural religion. We can act benevolently out of nature, which is fundamentally good, because of our creation by God. Friedrich Schleiermacher grounded ethics in a consciousness of God derived not from reason but from experience. For Søren Kierkegaard, God is the one beyond the ethical. We reach God through a leap of faith rather than by rational concepts.

Seventeenth- and eighteenth-century science and reason shaped a secular ethic, and theological reaction emphasized the role of experience.

In eighteenth-century Britain, the Industrial Revolution opened new moral questions. Emerging technology left many feeling excluded not only by society but also by the Church of England. In response to the Industrial Revolution, preachers found themselves profoundly affected as they became aware of the underside of societal change. John and Charles Wesley and George Whitefield preached powerfully about a justifying grace that transcends all status and spelled out requirements for a self-disciplined life. In New England, Jonathan Edwards preached that self-interest (so important in the development of capitalism) is inadequate. The social gospel movement of the late nineteenth and early twentieth centuries reacted further to the Industrial Revolution by opposing the greed of capitalism and appealing to the wealthy to show compassion and social responsibility for those in poverty. Later, Reinhold Niebuhr critiqued this movement as being naïve about sin. Beyond both utopian and pessimistic views of human nature, Niebuhr saw love in terms of selfless regard for others and connected this love with justice. Ethics, we are reminded, can be significantly shaped by economic and other social developments.

Over the last fifty years the voices of liberationist ethics (whether in Latin America, among racial minorities, or among women) have emphasized both personal experience and the historical forces and structures that oppress. Moral discourse is related to language, economics, and politics. Thus, social location needs to be acknowledged, and social power addressed. Ecumenism provides an arena for repentance and a constructive forum for addressing issues such as apartheid, nuclear disarmament, planetary sustainability, and marginality.[19] Again, preachers are called to wrestle with an ongoing ethical dialogue.

ETHICAL CHALLENGES FOR THE PREACHER		
From Culture	**From Scripture**	**From Church History**
Possible patenting of human embryos Increased legalized gambling Sexual immorality Pollution of the planet Euthanasia Capital punishment	Seemingly positive narratives with negative outcomes (e.g., Gen. 47) Economic arrangements in the Sabbath year (Deut. 15) The chosenness of Israel versus the universal scope of the gospel Law and grace in both testaments	How can one be sure who is really committed to the way of Christ rather than just expediently so? (fourth century) When the church loses its way, what then? (sixteenth century) What happens when science and reason shape a secular ethic? (seventeenth and eighteenth centuries) How did the Puritan preachers and the social gospel movement respond to industrialization? How do preachers grapple with the myriad of twentieth-century cries for liberation?

Obviously, outlining the questions that arise from culture, scripture, and the history of the church can feel overwhelming when we pile them up, as we have in the preceding pages. Sermons must avoid this avalanche style and treat questions in reasonable doses. But raising questions is important. In the following chapters more questions are lifted up than answers given. Leaving questions hanging for the congregation to mull over can be helpful, but eventually the preacher needs to indicate how the church can respond to moral issues. Wrestling with the issues of culture, scripture, and history may tempt the preacher to neglect the main task of preaching–inculcating the grand narrative of God's creating, sustaining, and redeeming activity. Out of this awareness listeners develop the ability to discern moral direction for discipleship. By hearing the Word faithfully proclaimed, the congregation is also formed as a moral community committed to following the way of Jesus Christ in obedience and hope.

> *The main task of preaching is inculcating the narrative of God's redeeming activity to nourish a congregation committed to the way of Jesus.*

A Christian Ethic in a Secular Society

In addition to facing questions from culture, scripture, and the history of the church, the Christian preacher is faced with the reality of a secular society, which surrounds the life of the church. To enable a congregation to live out of a *Christian* ethic means giving attention to the difference between Christian and secular ethics.

Is God Needed?

In a secular society no single way of thinking shapes how people view reality. Neither does a single way of thinking control their behavior.[20] When such a society rejects significant religious influence, its way of thinking can become a kind of practical atheism (even when people say they believe in some deity). Robert Buckman, president of the Canadian Humanist Association, argues that human beings don't need to make reference to any deity. It is sufficient to seek to live a useful life between birth and death. He acknowledges that some people affirm belief in God, but they do so for neurological reasons. "What is sometimes experienced as the voice of god or gods is associated with a particular area of the brain, programmed to go into relief mode when it encounters something it does not understand."[21]

The Christian Starting Point

Christians take a very different approach to moral discourse. Our starting point is God, not ourselves as scientists and philosophers have defined us–not our own views of right and wrong. Seeking God's way reshapes how we view the world and ourselves in it. If "the earth is the LORD's" (Ps. 24:1), then God is the ultimate owner, and our culture's view of property is seriously circumscribed. Our view of human life also changes the way we speak about its beginning and its ending. This, in turn, affects discussions of abortion and euthanasia. Similarly, when we engage issues raised by genetic research, we evaluate them in terms of our theology of humanness, our being made in the image of God. Theology forces us into a critical encounter with society's implicit values and how those values are grounded (or left ungrounded).

> *The Christian starting point is God, and seeking God's way shapes how we view the world.*

What is missing from contemporary secular ethical discussion, according to MacIntyre, is a sense of a larger purpose for being. In examining the novels of Jane Austen, MacIntyre argues that these narratives are ironic comedy rather than tragedy because, as a Christian, "she sees the *telos* of human life implicit in its everyday human form."[22] This future orientation gives life both purpose and meaning. Its loss is what has left our culture devoid of direction, wandering without any real ability to engage in substantive moral discourse. While Buckman and other humanists limit their ethics to the space between birth and death, Christians see their stories within a transcendent canvas beyond both.

> *Through the worship and preaching of the church, God is placed front and center.*

David Buttrick reminds us that "preaching alters identity by prefacing all our stories and setting them in a larger story that stretches back to the dawn of God's creation." Preaching also "conjures up an end to our stories," giving us a narrative mystery because it sketches "The Ending," that is, "the denouement of God's story with us." In this way, "Christian preaching poses the possibility of faith" that our lives are "related to the purposes of God that span human history."[23] We are given a sense that God is with us incarnate in Jesus Christ, who through the Holy Spirit enables our moral journey.

> *All our stories are within God's larger story, giving us a new beginning and a new ending and reminding us that God is always with us.*

The Preacher's Struggle

Faith in Christ makes all the difference to ethics. But we should not underestimate the extent to which preachers and congregations struggle with what it means to believe. On the one hand, in seeking to make preaching attractive, preachers may offer certitude rather than encourage faith.[24] This desire to be sure is itself a kind of defense against the onslaught of secularity. On the other hand, many allow themselves to feel acutely the questions that tragedy and other experiences pose. They wonder if they can continue to believe in God. One thinks of Elie Wiesel's portrayal of the death of a young boy in a Nazi prison camp and the question of an onlooker, "Where is God now?"[25] Such moments are devastating—like a sudden earthquake that demolishes a city. Who can fathom a purpose behind it all?

The fundamental difference between ethics that seeks to be Christian and one that does not can be discerned by going all the way back to the ancient Greek philosopher Socrates. For him, the good life concerns living morally. Because only such a life has meaning, he is prepared to die for it. Careful reflection asks what norms or appeals are adequate in particular circumstances to help one live morally. This is ethics according to Socrates.[26]

The Christian Difference

Christian ethics is different. It requires that all ethical thinking and acting revolve around Jesus of Nazareth, recognized as the crucified and risen Christ. So Christian ethics begins by taking into account what God has done in human history in Jesus Christ.[27] Of course, the term *Christian* with regard to ethics can be subdivided into Roman Catholic, Reformed, Evangelical, Liberal Protestant, and so forth.

In the 1930s Reinhold Niebuhr argued for "an independent Christian ethic" that moves beyond the "modern mind" and inadequate "Christian" responses to it.[28] The distinctive contribution of prophetic Christianity (as he calls it) lies in its comprehension of depth. Secular ethics deals with surfaces: resolving conflicts of interest and appealing to prudence and moderation. A Christian ethic rightly understood, says Niebuhr, probes what lies under forces of conflict and how they relate to the ultimate purpose in life. A Christian ethic moves beyond values to questions of good and evil. It moves beyond objectives to a more far-reaching hope.[29] A Christian ethic must question why, for example, a union might prevent an exploration of inappropriate behavior or why a company would reduce staff in ways that are dehumanizing? How would Christian decision-making, shaped by a larger vision of human well-being, lead to different actions from those who would operate out of a secular ethic? The preacher is called to help the congregation focus on the claims and liberties of the gospel of Christ and to lead them through a reflective process to come to an understanding of what it means to be a community of God's people.

> *Christian ethics is centered on what God has done in human history in Jesus Christ and on God's ultimate purposes.*

The Model: Ethics as an Interconnected Web

Many in the church, if they know anything about ethics at all, assume that ethics is primarily about norms and standards. What is right? What is wrong? How do you decide? Certainly, norms and standards are integral to ethical reflection. This study wants to challenge preachers and congregations to go beyond this and see ethics in its more complex form. We, therefore, propose a multifaceted approach. Such an approach seeks to create a broader view that will enable preaching to shape and nurture moral engagement. We *explore five elements of a more comprehensive ethical method:*

1. faith
2. moral character
3. norms
4. particularities of situation, context, and worldview
5. appeals to authority[30]

This is not the only way of engaging in moral reflection. Some ethicists focus primarily on norms, or on moral character, or on the consequences of decisions and actions. This is a reminder to preachers not to underestimate the possibilities that spring from interconnectedness.[31] But this theory of ethics holds particular promise for preaching. We will seek to demonstrate that preaching that uses this model can shape ethical understanding and moral behavior in many different ways and collectively can have significant impact when faithfully rooted in the gospel of Jesus Christ. Because these elements are all related to one another, we present it using the image of an interconnected web.

The Web's Interconnections

In this interconnected web each aspect of ethical reflection is affected by each of the others. To believe, to trust in Jesus Christ (*faith*), shapes us individually and collectively (*moral character*), and both influence our approach to what we discern as God's requirements (*norms*). These in turn affect how we look at particular moral issues (*situation and context*). How we appeal to such things as experience or scripture (*authority*) bears on our analysis of specific situations that we encounter. These can function in a different order. We may begin

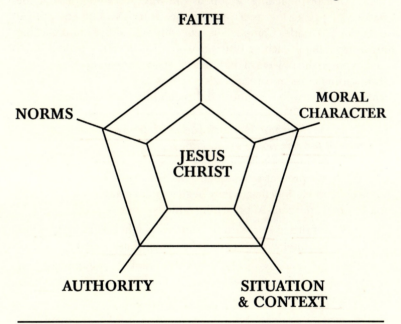

Interconnected Ethical Web for Preaching

with authoritative sources or with the particulars of a given situation. We could move from moral character to basic convictions. Each element in ethical reflection reverberates with the others, though sometimes less obviously.[32]

Evolving the web metaphor into the cyberspace image of the World Wide Web of the Internet suggests that many dimensions of preaching ethics move well beyond what can be seen from the pulpit. We note that the movement on the WWW can begin at any station. So with sermons, listeners always bring (perhaps not always consciously) their faith, their situations, their character, their sense of norms, and their understandings of authority into the pew with them. The WWW also reminds us, with Barbara Brown Taylor, that we live in an interconnected world that can be described as *a luminous web*. We belong, she says, "to a web of creation in which nothing, absolutely nothing, is inconsequential."[33] Taylor's remarks remind us not to underestimate the possibilities that spring from interconnectedness.

Jesus as the Web's Center

Jesus Christ is the luminous center of our web. The earliest Christian credo was "Jesus Christ is Lord." When this becomes the focal point of preaching, it "opens the way for us to consider the nature of preaching as a part of the church's obedient ethical behavior."[34] Charles Campbell has cogently argued that our preaching arises from the preaching of Jesus, who incarnated the word of God and exposed the powers of darkness, effecting redemption from them through his cross and resurrection.[35] It is essential that each of the stations on our web is connected through him to each other.

Jesus, the incarnate Word, embodies his own preaching and ours at the very center of our ethical web.

While we present our sequence as a heuristic device, students, preachers, and homileticians may begin employing these steps toward a full-orbed approach to preaching ethics.

(1) With **faith** as our starting point, we might ask, How does this or that intersect with or challenge our basic beliefs?

(2) When we focus on who we are as part of a community of faith (our **moral character**), we could ask, How does our character shape our approach to this issue?

(3) This paves the way for us to explore Christian behavior (our **obligations** before God), with the question, How is our relationship before God reflected in what we are doing?

(4) When we examine **situations and contexts,** we do so with an awareness of the larger frameworks at work in our thinking: What exactly is actually going on here, and how is our perception of it affected by the world around us?

(5) We probe the **sources of authority** to which we appeal by asking, To what are we appealing when we express our viewpoints?

Even while following this sequence, preachers will want to distinguish between a reflective process for looking at ethical dimensions of preaching ethics and homiletical decisions as to which of these becomes a part of the sermon and how. The selection and order need to be appropriate to each particular sermon. The shape of that sermon arises from other factors, such as the biblical text, a theological theme, a moral issue, or the best way to communicate one or another of these in a given setting.

Aspects of Faith

In anticipation of what we explore in the following chapters, we turn now to look briefly at our five aspects of ethics.

Faith

What, as Christians and as a community of believers, do we fundamentally believe? What are our most basic convictions about God, our world, and ourselves? How do these help clarify for us what is right or wrong? What is our view of life, the source of our hope? To be followers of Jesus Christ is to live out what we believe about him. More than that, it is, with the apostle Paul, to let Christ live through us, to live by faith in him (Gal. 2:20).

What we believe and how we trust God shapes our ethics, the standards we seek to live by, the kind of persons we strive to be, and our perception of reality around us. We explicitly or implicitly start with faith and keep on returning to it by asking, Now, what is it again that we as disciples of Christ believe, and whom do we trust? So, for example, Ken Kim, a missionary in Guatemala, was prepared to put his own life on the line to help a widow seek ways to discover who murdered her husband. Trust in God's providence guided his ethical search for justice. In chapter 2 we bring the kinds of theological convictions we have noted above to explore how preaching can assist congregations to reflect as a Christian community on a number of moral questions.

> *What we believe and how we trust God shapes our ethics.*

Moral Character

As moral persons, who are we called and enabled to be? What sort of community is the church meant to be? How does being "a new creation" in Christ (2 Cor. 5:17) affect our characters, our personalities, our attitudes? Our witness in the world is significantly furthered or contradicted by what kind of persons and what sort of community we are. When Matthew Lukwiya, the highly trained Ugandan Christian medical doctor, courageously helped his hospital staff cope with the deadly Ebola virus, he knew the risks. But before succumbing himself, he confessed, "When we serve with love, that is when the risk does not matter so much."[36] Christian character is formed when preachers tell such stories of people who have so clearly chosen to live out their faith. Chapter 3 considers what we understand by moral integrity, the term *virtuous* in relation to the professions, our new humanity in Christ, and the character traits given to us by the Spirit.

> *Who we are as Christians and as Christian communities shapes our moral attitudes and behavior.*

our behavior reveals what we believe.

NORMS

Those who seek to follow Christ seek an ethic of grateful response and yearn for normative standards, principles, values, and rights to clarify their discipleship. All of these are aspects of the ethics of doing, of living out what we believe. If we look at the normative principle of stewardship (especially as expressed in Lev. 25), we note that recently it has inspired Christians to connect globally in support of reducing the debt of the poorest countries of the world. In chapter 4 we turn to scripture passages that spell out the ethic of obligation, explore the fundamental principles, and examine how values and rights bear on attitudes toward such things as corporate social responsibility and human relatedness.

SITUATION AND CONTEXT

Moral questions emerge in particular situations that we find ourselves in and are, in turn, set in larger social, political, and cultural contexts. When two aboriginal women were asked about why the children in their community were sniffing glue and committing suicide, they pointed to the way their culture has been undermined by residential schools. To explore such moral issues requires gathering information, analyzing the data with the help of the social sciences, and evaluating the results from the perspective of faith. It also means probing the worldviews of both native and non-native communities as each seeks to respond. Preaching, as Martin Luther King Jr. pointed out, is calling people to see beyond their limited horizons, to discern (and begin to enter) God's alternative order for humankind. This process of gathering information and then analyzing and evaluating the data gathered (through the perspective of Christian convictions) provides the agenda of chapter 5.

> *Moral questions arise in particular situations and contexts that require gathering data and then analyzing and evaluating it from a Christian perspective.*

AUTHORITY

Moral actions and arguments may appeal to particular underlying authorities, including scripture, reason, tradition, and experience. How we understand authorization may involve interpretation or appeals to specialized studies. How these are weighted and whether they reveal something new or testify in fresh ways to the biblical revelation in Jesus Christ are matters debated by ethicists.[37] Discussions about abortion may appeal to the experience of women, the tradition of the church, or biblical passages such as Genesis 1:26–27; Exodus 21:22–23; Jeremiah 1:4–5; and Matthew 1:18–23.

The preacher recognizes this complexity and also the fact that in an imperfect world the ideal may not always be attained. Chapter 6 explores the ways in which narratives of experience and empirical studies, the gift of wisdom (including science), the influence of church tradition, and ways of interpreting scripture are related to ethical reflection and action.

> *Sources of authority to which we often appeal in ethical discourse are scripture, tradition, reason, and experience.*

Homiletical Assumptions and Preliminary Observations about Preaching

We have acknowledged some of the many questions that confront preachers and congregations, and sketched a particular way of looking at ethical reflection. Now we turn to some homiletical assumptions as we focus on *the preaching of ethics*. This includes the kinds of homiletical forms that might best communicate the various aspects of ethics that we have outlined.

In recent years preaching has evolved in a number of significant ways. Fred Craddock and others who proposed inductive, narrative, imaginative, and more congregation-centered sermons challenged the deductive, three-point sermon of the 1950s. Sermons, they said, have to appeal not only to the understanding but also to the heart and to the imagination.³⁸ Preaching that moves beyond abstractions and explanations can draw congregations into the experience of the text and the world of the sermon. As a preacher and teacher of preaching, I have appropriated much of this and am particularly indebted to many people, mostly in the Academy of Homiletics. For me, preaching is a theological exercise involving serious engagement with scripture as witness to Jesus Christ through whom we invite congregations to see the world and its principalities in both their fallenness and their manifestations of grace.³⁹ To nurture ethical formation in such a world, preaching may take many forms, depending on what is happening in the lives of both the preacher and the congregation, the chosen biblical texts, the particular aspects of ethical reflection selected, and any moral issue under consideration.

> ***Central to preaching is theology and serious engagement with scripture as witness to Jesus Christ through whom we invite congregations to see the world and its principalities in both their fallenness and their manifestations of grace.***

This raises a number of questions for the preacher:

1. If preaching uses interpretation, explanation, inspiration, narrative, challenge, encouragement, calling to action, reassurance, exploring particular facts, and the like, which of these might be most appropriate for conveying a given aspect of moral reflection?

2. Preachers often expect the biblical text to shape the thrust and creativity of the sermon. Frequently, the lectionary reading, usually the gospel, takes the lead. How does this assumption affect preaching ethics? This book presumes that biblically oriented preaching and preaching ethics nourish each other. The sermon, Walter Brueggemann reminds us, is where a new community is weekly being convened. This is a crucial event not only for the church but also for society. "We must interpret to live. There is almost no other voice left to do interpretation on which society depends that is honest, available and open to criticism." This is "a public event in which society reflects on what and who it will be."⁴⁰ The sermon is an ethical moment. Sometimes moral issues (such as genetic engineering, poverty and wealth, or abusive behavior) may be directly included in sermons, but preachers

may also contribute to ethical awareness and moral formation by faithfully exploring the thrust of a text to illuminate what faith is and how it is to be lived.

3. Does the congregation participate in preaching? If, with Stanley Hauerwas, we see "the church as a community capable of sustaining a distinctive moral vision of the world," then the congregation brings a great deal to the sermon. For example, in the decisions of an established congregation in a declining urban setting, ethical discovery arises out of very practical decisions that require interpretation and liturgical celebration. The preacher plays a mediating role so that the congregation understands its ethical engagement.[41]

These sorts of homiletical explorations are woven with concrete examples through subsequent chapters. The final chapter probes what it means to apply ethical reflection directly to preacher as proclaimer of ethics, sermon as ethical communication, and listening congregation as ethical community. Preaching does not carry all the freight of the reflective process. It has its limits and its partners, and these will be acknowledged as we pursue the particular possibilities of the sermon for ethics.

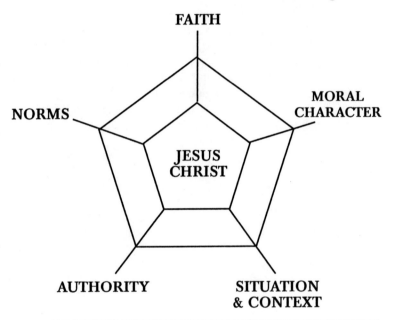

Interconnected Ethical Web for Preaching

2

FAITH

Preaching a Gospel Perspective

Preaching Christian ethics assumes a commitment to *Christian* faith. To preach to a community of the baptized is to let faith intentionally shape its language and perspective. A preacher's listeners are "God's own people" (1 Pet. 2:9). This means the church belongs to another and seeks to live out of that belonging.[1] So the congregation listens to preaching differently from those who do not share baptismal commitment. God's people expect to hear the gospel of Christ and let gospel theology form and guide their ethics.

In this chapter we explore the first element in the process of ethical reflection for preaching. We focus on the relationship of gospel *faith* to moral issues. We seek to answer the basic ethical question, How does a given moral question intersect with or challenge our basic beliefs? We answer the question in four steps, pausing at each step to focus on a contemporary moral issue.

1. We begin with the obvious **foundation statement:** What we believe as Christians frames our whole experience of preaching. Gospel faith shapes the church's way of viewing the world.[2]

2. Next, we look specifically at **our understanding of God,** our need to experience God's presence, and our sense of divine

providence. As a test case for our model, we ponder how these doctrines of faith shape the way we look at the morality of legalized gambling.
3. We turn to **our doctrine of human nature,** specifically the fact that we are made in the image of God. This leads us to reflect on how to respond as people of faith to the ethical issues raised by our culture's interests in genetic research.
4. Finally, we focus on **our convictions about sin, repentance, and forgiveness.** From this standpoint we shine the gospel spotlight on the moral problem of domestic violence. That light forces us to grapple with our convictions and to explore some assumptions about what we believe repentance involves and forgiveness requires.

As we work our way through these reflections, we keep noting implications for preaching.

Ethics and Gospel Faith

In 1993 Croatian theologian Miroslav Volf was in Germany lecturing on loving one's neighbor. When he finished, the renowned German theologian Jurgen Moltmann asked him a searing ethical question: "But can you embrace a *cetnik*?" Both knew whom he meant by *cetniks*. They were Serbian fighters who had ravished Croatia, committing widespread rape and murder. To Croatians they were "the ultimate other." Volf's response was utterly candid, "No, I cannot—but as a follower of Christ I should be able to." The moral dilemma for him was clear. He felt that his "faith was at odds with itself, divided between the God who delivers the needy and the God who abandons the Crucified, between the demand to bring about justice for the victims and the call to embrace the perpetrator." This ethical struggle led him to write his penetrating analysis of reconciliation, *Exclusion and Embrace.*[3] Here, faith wrestles with hatred of the other, so pervasive in our world, and calls for a radical alternative. This is, then, the first step in examining the intersection of faith and moral issues.

Theology and Cultural Agendas

A theology of reconciliation challenges cultural "law and order" retaliation agendas. This challenge has far-reaching implications for how the sermon tackles deep, emotion-laden problems such as the appropriate response to the terrorist attacks on New York, Washington, and Pennsylvania in the fall of 2001. Gospel reconciliation helps the preacher move beyond the pull of patriotism because its view of God transcends all political and military supremacy while its view of human nature reminds us that evil is pervasive in the world that stands in need of a Savior. Facing such moral issues, we must explore again what we believe. Like Volf, when we dig into what we believe, we often see ourselves called to an ethic different from what we had assumed and had practiced. This theological disposition energizes us—as preachers and as congregation—to explore the church's long debate between just war theory and pacifism.[4]

> *Theology rooted in the reconciling action of Christ enables preaching to engage events such as 9/11 with hope well beyond patriotism.*

Such theological exploration raises a double question for the preacher: Will our preaching be ethically faithful to the gospel, and will the congregation embrace this life-changing news as people of faith? To think as a Christian, says Mark Noll in a frank self-reflection, is a disciplined task. Our failure to exercise our minds for Christ on matters such as "the nature and workings of the physical world" and "the character of human social structures like government and the economy" has become acute. I would add that this is even more difficult when pondering retaliatory actions that seek to define justice primarily in terms of vengeance. Noll names this "the scandal of the evangelical mind."[5] So how might a preacher help a congregation turn aside this scandal and think about moral questions as a baptized community?

BAPTIZED INTO A NEW COMMUNITY

In the course of leading a workshop on ethics a couple of years ago, I asked a church group to consider a painful, very personal question. I asked, "What would you do if your father or mother were seriously ill and begging for help in ending his or her life?" Supposing, I said, that you could give one pill to ease the pain or two to end life. What would you do and why?[6] The group was divided. Some could not help end another's life; others felt they should respect a parental plea. Then I asked, "Does what we believe as Christians make a difference in how we should respond to this question?" In this way participants were invited to reflect on the relationship between faith and ethics. I could also have said that such decision-making is one way of living out our baptism, our inauguration into the way of Jesus Christ. Preachers learn a lot about how to speak about faith in relation to ethics by having this sort of discussion.

> ***To be baptized into Christ is to be part of a community that is committed to seeking the way of Jesus Christ, even when this challenges cultural values.***

Of course, societal contexts also influence congregations. This is not new. God called the apostle Paul, the strictest of Jews, to communicate the gospel to Gentile communities across the Roman Empire. The gospel message itself had been deeply rooted in Jewish communities. Paul had to find new forms of discourse to translate the saving message into this new Gentile context.[7] This involves more than taking seriously the particular circumstances of a congregation and its surrounding neighborhood. It includes the very language, thought forms, and values of the surrounding culture, even though much of this is not always at the level of consciousness. Out of this contextual awareness the sermon gives listeners the distinctive language of faith that helps them discern the often limited perspective of their culture.

A culture-conscious congregation may decide to live out its baptism as a morally conscious community. Even then the congregation faces challenges. Attempts to incarnate Christian moral teachings too often "degenerate into legalism, single-issue politics, captivity to one side or another in current culture wars, or dancing with divergent ideologies that divide them internally and undermine their public credibility." In making this observation Lewis Mudge adds, "there is little consensus among the churches about the *relationship* between faith as believed and sacramentally shared and the way congregations should understand themselves as moral communities in each place, let alone as members of a reconciling community that spans the globe."[8]

Additionally, our pervasively secular culture has removed the church from its accustomed place at the center of society. Indeed, morally speaking, society no longer has a center. This should not surprise nor hinder the church, for biblical faith was born at the margins of society. Jesus was crucified outside the gate. The history of the early church encourages us to see that the church on the margin and gifted by the Spirit should not be underestimated as a moral force in the world.[9] This is not to imply that the church is institutionally stronger than it really is. Rather, the church is linked to God's reign proclaimed in the parables of Jesus and established through his cross and resurrection. The only power of the church is the power of the gospel of Christ, and this is the moral force that will have the last word, as Handel reminds us in the recitative, "and He shall reign forever and ever."

> *We preach out of social marginality but also with confidence that the reign of God at the heart of Jesus' preaching enables risk and inspires hope.*

ETHICS AND GOD'S PRESENCE

Sometimes the risk a congregation takes is poignantly acute—as when inscrutable events emerge in our lives and in our world. A character in an Elie Wiesel novel is not the only person asking, Where is God? Listen closely. You will hear the same question raised quite frequently in the children's wards of our hospitals, at a family gathered to mourn a teenage bystander killed by a drunk driver, or in a community seeking ways to respond to a shocking hurricane that rips though Central American countries leaving devastation in its wake. When we look at these events or at the enormous economic and political disparities between communities and countries, how do we think about God? This *God question* is, then, the second step in examining the intersection of beliefs and moral issues.

GOD AS THEOLOGY'S PROBLEM

Theology's only problem, says Jürgen Moltmann, is *God*—and God is present, dwelling with us in *God's* kingdom.[10] In a secular culture it is all too easy to separate the world from God. But Moltmann reminds us that when we see the world in all its brokenness through the lens of theology, we can discern both the necessity for an alternative order (which Jesus describes in his parables of the kingdom of God)[11] and are reminded that transforming the world belongs to God. We are called in our preaching to be faithful witnesses to Christ.

Moltmann has challenged modern theology to revolutionize our world by incarnating what he calls a "theology of hope." He sees God as both suffering in Jesus Christ for the wounds and sins of the world and also affirming life and energizing hope. When the world loses a sense of God, it is no longer bothered by the suffering of others. Thus, science has made enormous contributions to human well-being, especially in the area of medicine, but it has also created instruments of mass destruction. Our hope finally lies not in what *we* can do, but in God's suffering presence, God's journeying with us.[12]

> *Preachers, reflecting on God's suffering presence in Jesus Christ, call not only their members but all in positions of power to exercise their military, economic, and cultural influence with humility and accountability.*

God alone authorizes the sermon. A God-authorized sermon becomes part of establishing the divine world order, God's kingdom. I know from personal experience how often I need to be reminded that the preaching task is a sacred trust, one engaged only in the crucible of prayer. Only by bowing before the One who calls us to preach are we released into the freedom to do so as God's servants. But how can I discern whether I have been faithful to God's call? Often this requires reflecting back on what has been preached. It also calls forth confidence in the congregation's spiritual discernment. Those who long to hear a word from the Lord listen differently, and the effect on the preacher can be palpable. While the ethical impact of our preaching often seems hard to measure, listeners, given a chance to give feedback, can often say when our preaching is too vague or timid and when and how it really enables someone to act in a moral way.

LEGALIZED GAMBLING–LOST SENSE OF GOD'S PRESENCE

Seeing ethics as part of God's world order releases us to face tough moral questions raised by our secular culture. As a case in point, we will look at one modern issue facing the church: How does legalized gambling intersect with or challenge our basic beliefs? The answer to this question rests on solutions to other queries: How is the congregation influenced by its surrounding culture? How can preaching on God's providence provide a critical perspective on this phenomenon?

The astounding increase in legalized gambling across North America in the past few decades, particularly in the 1990s, should raise the church's moral antennae. What does this element of secular society signify for the church? Does it show that inside and outside the church people lack any awareness of God's strong role in their lives? Does it mean that those who buy lottery tickets or visit casinos don't ask themselves about how this relates to their view of the world and God? Does this represent a total divorce between faith and actions?

The secular news assertion, "We've become a nation of gamblers,"[13] should give us pause. Various recent reports indicate that the Government of the Province of Ontario (population about twelve million) has *net* gambling revenues of $2.34 billion annually. This amount comes out of a total gambling take of $5.47 billion[14] after all prizes and expenses are paid. Niagara Falls, an Ontario tourist city of less than eighty thousand, has become one of the main gambling centers of the province. It has casinos, video lottery terminals (VLTs), and other forms of gambling, one part of the lure that welcomed fourteen million visitors in 1997. In 2000 this one small city alone took in more than $2 billion in gambling.[15]

This is not a benign sport. Ontario has almost one hundred thousand pathological gamblers and twice as many problem gamblers on the way to becoming pathologically addicted. Ontario spends only 1 percent of its net revenue to assist these people. Social costs, of course, are not only monetary; they include dysfunctional workers, disrupted families, loss of homes, mental breakdown, and even suicides. In 1988 only two U.S. states permitted casinos. Ten years later that number rose to twenty-three. In 1994 Americans wagered $482 billion. David Phillips, a sociologist, has shown that in this time frame suicide rates increased considerably. Visitors to Las Vegas are two and a half times more likely to die by their own hand than visitors to non-gambling cities. Suicide rates also increased in Atlantic City and Reno after casinos arrived.[16]

Gambling works on the principle that to enable *one or two* people to *win* millions of dollars, *hundreds of thousands* of people have to *lose* many more millions. Why, then, do about 80 percent of Canadians participate in some form of gambling? Why do governments legalize and advertisers promote what is patently destructive behavior? The following factors are often noted: Gambling mirrors high-risk international currency and stock trading. A *me-first* kind of individualism diminishes the value of the common good. Businesses and the entertainment industry successfully promote greed.[17] It is interesting to note that greed has long been considered a vice, but is now being promoted almost as a virtue–a striking moral reversal!

Beneath all these factors, some writers point to worship of the goddess Fortuna. An editorial in *The Christian Century* links lotteries with the view that "life is a series of gambits that can always be overturned by the roll of the dice." Such a view weakens our sense of the value of our daily investments in work, family, and community. Our resolve to oppose inequality and unfairness diminishes. The tragic consequences of gambling don't matter much any more. The theological consequences are ignored but still real. The various forms of "gambling trivialize and attempt to manipulate God's providence–God's order and care of creation." Rather than believe that God's hand is on our lives for a purpose, gamblers trust the roll of the cosmic dice. Trust Lady Luck; accept the enigmatic guidance of the goddess Fortuna.[18] Faith is replaced by superstition and homage to a false deity who teases with a big win that virtually never happens.

> **Rather than believe that God's hand is on our lives for a purpose, gamblers trust the roll of the cosmic dice.**

Getting accurate numerical facts on ethical issues is important. They let us see the problems intellectually. Personal stories provide another type of important data. They help us feel the experience of addiction. A mother speaks out about her son, who was hooked on VLTs and committed suicide. "He tried to beat the addiction several times during the nine years that he played VLTs. However, in the end—unable to even seek help from the ones who cared for him the most—he took his own life. It was six weeks before his twenty-sixth birthday." Stories, like statistics, need analysis and interpretation. This mother quotes the president of the Canadian Psychiatric Association: "Addiction to gambling is the fastest growing psychiatric disorder in North America."[19]

Beyond illness lies greed, forcing a choice to be made between God and Fortuna. In Matthew 6 Jesus pointed out the precariousness of accumulating wealth and invited his listeners to trust the providence of God: "Look at the flowers of the field and the birds of the air. God takes care of each one of them, and God values you even more. Strive first for the kingdom of God and everything else will fall into place" (vv. 28–33, paraphrased). This is a teleological perspective.[20] There is a larger story—God's story. Set within that divine kingdom context, our life-journeys are secure. As we experience God's presence and love, getting for ourselves at the expense of others gives way to sharing and genuine caring.

The Preacher's Process

All of this moves in the right direction—caring for others rather than just pleasing ourselves. But in practice, preachers may move in a different direction. They may be so angry about the legalized gambling movement as a force of evil that the congregation only hears condemnation. They also need to hear a word of grace. The gospel, of course, condemns the evil implicit in gambling, but it does so most profoundly at the cross, the source of hope as well. Gambling is based on a false optimism, a principal cause of despair in Western societies. Through the prism of the cross, the sermon invites the congregation to see how God meets the world's despair, brokenness, and competitiveness with a transforming love that faces rather than evades reality.[21]

The **homiletical process** here includes several elements:

1. **Becoming informed** about a large social issue (the statistics and commentaries on legalized gambling)
2. **Allowing ourselves to feel** it at the personal level (the mother's story)
3. **Moving to an alternative, Christian perspective** on life (Jesus' comments in Matthew)
4. **Thinking theologically** about the contrast between looking at life as though God doesn't exist versus seeing ourselves as loved and cared for by God
5. Being careful **to center the sermon in the gospel** rather than fall into the trap of judgmental superiority

In a world that does not take sin seriously, exploring the way in which greed builds on anxiety and moves toward the rejection of God could be profoundly helpful. This would call for more of an expository sermon, but such a sermon would need to be concretized with reference to manifestations of greed.[22]

Ethics and God's Image

Our third step in examining the intersection of beliefs and moral issues moves us from the God question to the issue of *human nature*. We affirm in faith that we are made in the image of God (Gen. 1:26–28) and stand in a covenantal relationship with God and the rest of God's creation. The covenantal relationship rests on divine initiative, not human action. This article of faith forms the ground for Christian self-understanding.

Psalm 8 is a hymn to God that arose from reflection on these verses in Genesis. The psalmist realized the paradox of our creatureliness. The inspired writer looked at the vastness of the stars and planets, thought of God's awesome power, and asked, "What are human beings that you [God] are mindful of them?" He then declared that we have been made just a little below divine beings (see note to v. 5 in NRSV). Human finitude is recognized, but we are not lost in the vastness of space. We are exalted to the special role of God's royal stewards, given responsibility like that of a shepherd to care for all nonhuman creatures and, by implication, their habitat. Jesus Christ embodies and displays the full potential of this humanity (Eph. 1:16–23).[23]

Individual and Social Dimensions

To be created in the image of God includes both individual and social dimensions. When we stress that God is One, we emphasize our individual spirituality. To concentrate on God as Trinity is to recognize our social interconnectedness. We may be inclined by an individualistic culture to favor the former, but God's sociality reminds us of our own. Each of us is uniquely loved by God and also created for relationship.[24]

> *To be created in God's image shapes an understanding of human nature that respects both our individuality and our connectedness with one another and with God's whole creation.*

This theological picture contrasts with two contemporary perspectives in secular culture. The first perspective sees human beings as simply units in some larger social whole. Our purpose is our usefulness to that collective entity. We are nothing more than commodities to be owned by others. The second view, that of liberal individualism, sees each person as an autonomous, self-sustaining, separate self.[25] This makes us proprietors of our own lives; we own our bodies and are free to think whatever we want. Both of these modern notions of the self are thoroughly secular—severed from relationship with God and, therefore, distorting both our individuality and our sociality.

In 1997 the World Alliance of Reformed Churches met in Debrecen, Hungary, and sought to answer two questions: (1) Who are we as human beings, and (2) Who are we as church? To do this, the conference utilized the answer to question 1 of the *Heidelberg Catechism*, "We belong body and soul, in life and in death—not to ourselves but to our faithful Savior Jesus Christ." Confessing theological and moral failures, asking for forgiveness, and claiming the new life that forgiveness makes possible, the Declaration uses the refrain *"we are not our own"* to spell out ethical implications:

1. We are stewards.
2. No human ideology holds the secret to history.
3. No one should be excluded.
4. Human beings are not commodities.

5. A simple lifestyle witnesses to God's ordering.
6. We do not despair, for God reigns.
7. With the whole people of God, we proclaim: *Soli Deo Gloria!*[26]

Here, theology and ethics meet in a clear and compelling proclamation that is both Christian and dramatically countercultural. We may best see this intersection by looking at another ethical issue raised by modern culture, that of genetic research.

HUMAN NATURE AND GENETIC RESEARCH

This image-of-God theology has profound implications for genetic inquiry. But how does a Christian understanding of human nature probe the ethical side of genetic research? Here is another moral question that intersects with what we believe. We reflect on this question in the context of our society's three quite different perspectives of science. For some, human beings are merely biological entities, and science holds the clue to meaning. For others, life is pure mystery. Science should not interfere with the natural course of life. A third view recognizes the value of scientific knowledge but sees life as more than biology. This group acknowledges a sacred nonbiological human spirit.[27] Among the listening congregation, each perspective could seem at least somewhat plausible—though perhaps more as an inclination than a conviction.

In chapter 1 we raised this question of genetic research with reference to cloning and patent applications that had the potential to treat life as a commodity. At a deeper theological level we also posed the question of who "owns" life. If God is the creator of life, then how do Christians view the patenting of life forms?

This question was raised again in the Supreme Court of Canada, which ruled in December 2002 that a genetically modified mouse developed by two Harvard University scientists and called the "Oncomouse" was not an invention and therefore should not be patented in Canada. The Canadian Council of Churches used this occasion to help churches explore the larger area of genetic research. The Council report notes that the Supreme Court argued that the patent application is based on a metaphysical view that nature is simply composed of data subject to human manipulation. This, the court said, objectifies the natural world; and, because humans are part of nature, it would inevitably objectify them. While the lawyers for the Harvard scientists argued that theological and ethical issues are not relevant to an interpretation of patent law, the Court decided otherwise.[28]

> *The Supreme Court of Canada said that to patent a genetically modified mouse assumes that nature is open to manipulation, and it could lead to objectifying human beings.*

Guidelines for Churches

In reflecting on how churches can think ethically on such an issue, Richard Crossman offers a series of guidelines to help churches make responsible judgments in the area:

1. Clarify the relationship between the ends and the means in research.
2. Recognize that stewardship is not ownership.
3. Challenge misleading rhetoric about biological advances and promises.
4. Affirm the dignity of life as God-given.
5. Make ethical decisions as part of a community.
6. Remember that, as Christians, we need not defy and defer death at all costs.[29]

Of course, many other questions are related to this complex subject of biotechnology. How widely do we define genetically inherited disease? Will we end up diminishing the diversity of the human gene pool? If so, what does this risk? How will information from genetic screening be used? Could genetic screening have monetary implications (e.g., in the area of insurance coverage)?[30] These questions remind us further of the complexity and moral edges of genetic research.[31] To find answers requires both the special knowledge and experience of genetic experts and the critical angle of vision that connects human life with God. Many scientists accept this position and desire to work with it in their research and in conversation with communities of faith. The church must provide theologians with sufficient scientific training to enter into dialogue on these most pressing issues.[32]

In light of this brief engagement with biotechnology, preachers are reminded that:

1. They **begin with their theology,** specifically their understanding of creation and humanness.
2. A congregation can be helped to reflect theologically when a sermon spells out **society's differing perspectives and shows how they are related to faith.**

3. A major **event in the news** (such as the decision regarding the Oncomouse legal case) **provides an opportunity** to draw attention in a limited way to society's perspectives and how the church may reflect on them.

The ultimate goal of such preaching is a deepened sense of our God-connectedness that finally leads us with the psalmist to doxology. Praise has its own way of opening up a wider vision of reality.[33] This means that the form of the sermon may be not only explanation but also poetic utterance.

ETHICS AND HUMAN SIN

In examining the intersection of beliefs and moral issues, we have moved from the God question to the issue of human nature and now to the *problem of human sin*. The Christian church's theological creeds describe the fact of human sin, God's invitation to repentance, and God's offer of forgiveness. How do we view the world in light of this conviction? How can the church—composed as it is of repentant, forgiven sinners—become a morally responsible community? We begin with reflections on sin and see its connection with redemption in Christ. Then we reflect on confession of sin and forgiveness in relation to the issue of domestic violence.

No one can attend to the daily news and not be acutely aware that many aspects of life and many ways of running business or government are deeply flawed. Is it that we are simply not capable? Is it a matter of ignorance? Are individuals and institutions willfully misguided, even sometimes intentionally perverse? We are willing to overlook certain mistakes, but increasingly a litigious society seeks to lay greater blame and to discover more sinister motives. The flaws go deeper.

From a Christian perspective the world is not just weak and finite; it is fragmented, broken by sin. Charles Campbell has explored in great detail the biblical view of principalities and powers as spiritual forces influencing evil in the world.[34] Under the aegis of these powers human beings fail to trust in God and cause deep suffering and injustice.

Theology's Affirmations

Similarly, Terry Anderson reminds us of three affirmations of faith that help clarify ethical reflection about sin:[35]

1. Sin is an **awesome power that enslaves** us and our world; to overcome it we need a delivering power from beyond ourselves.

2. Sin is **both personal and social;** individuals and societies need redemption.
3. Sin is **persistent;** working out our salvation is an ongoing task.

Sin as an Awesome Power

If sin is confined to the individual, then the ethical issues become primarily a matter of individual moral choice. Holding this view, we will proclaim that Christ enables us to make right choices by the use of reason and by following his example. Individuals would be urged simply to choose more wisely. When this doesn't work, severely harsh laws may be enacted that do not get at the root cause of the problem. This perspective may thus miss the deeper dimensions of social wrongs.

For the apostle Paul, however, sin has the power to enslave human beings (Rom. 5:21; 6:17). If sin is enslavement, we will preach a cosmic Christ who has subjected all powers under himself (Col. 1:15–16). We are then reconciled through his death on the cross (Col. 1:22). Viewing sin as a cosmic power invading the world, we will also be more inclined to pursue questions of basic justice and fairness. The democratic process itself may reflect ways of checking the power of rulers who, because of the power of sin, may not rule justly.[36] The preacher needs to clarify assumptions about sin in this larger biblical perspective. This can be done through interpretation and with stories such as that of the Enron scandal. Such interpretation must carefully show more than individual failure on the part of CEOs; it must include how the market system itself became corrupted. People such as John Cassidy have demonstrated how regulatory changes allowed transparency to be cloaked and opened possible ways to limit accountability.[37]

Sin Is Both Personal and Social

Some time ago I was moved by a radio account of a remarkable event that occurred in the fall of 2000 in Switzerland. The world Jewish community was honoring a number of bureaucrats who had served in various European countries during World War II. These had been singled out because they had deliberately chosen not to follow the rules and had helped Jews to escape to freedom. Most of the bureaucrats had been demoted; some of them were killed. The son of one of them was asked about his father, who had lived as a pauper for the rest of his life and had recently died. The son, like the rest of his family, had also been deprived. His response was deep gratitude for his father's courage and faith. His father had done the right thing in a structure that was morally bankrupt.

In less dramatic ways one reads accounts of civil servants (in democratic countries such as the United States or Canada) under orders to remain silent even if they disagree with a given policy they are asked to implement. But sometimes they speak out because the wrongness of the system stands over against their conviction of what is right.[38] The preaching of the prophets of ancient Israel and the strange vision of the beast in Revelation 13 help us see the corporate nature of sin. The church needs to work for corporate changes as well as individual ones.

> *The corporate nature of evil calls for resistance even when this resistance is costly.*

But how might this corporate dimension of gospel proclamation be accomplished homiletically? In October of 1993 Philip Wogaman preached a sermon that essentially took the congregation on an imaginary tour of two streets in the city of Washington. Foundry United Methodist Church is at the corner where these streets intersect. On one street he kept on encountering people in need, so he called this the "Street of People." The other street was dotted with institutional offices with varying degrees of power: the National Rifle Association, the National Education Association, the union offices of the AFL-CIO, even the White House. This he named the "Street of Power." Toward the end of the tour Wogaman asked, "Is it the business of the church to be at this intersection of power and people?" His response was that the real intersection of these two streets "is in the life of God, God who is brooding over the hurt of the people in the streets, God who is challenging those who have responsibilities of power...to take responsibility before God for the well-being of God's children." The sermon ends with readings from scripture. Proverbs 31:8–9 commands that we speak out for those who cannot speak and defend the rights of the poor. The vision in Zechariah 8:4–5 pictures a God-transformed Jerusalem where the elderly are safe and the children can play.[39]

> *God is at the intersection of the streets of power and people and calls for prophetic speech.*

SIN IS PERSISTENT

To appreciate the persistence of sin, we need to see the connection between justification and sanctification. In Romans 8, Paul provided a careful exposition of the justifying grace of God. Then he attached his strongest exhortation to live by the Spirit. Life in the Spirit should be a life that resists sin, that is, a life of sanctification. Without the persistent sanctifying work of the Spirit, however, even a Christian holding high public office cannot give sanctified Christian leadership or provide ethically responsible service. Sin has the capacity to infiltrate political views and lead the executive away from public accountability. To account for this, some ethicists argue for more authority in corporate structures to ensure moral government. But sin's tenacity is not limited to the individual level. It afflicts corporate structures, too. Thus, a mediating position between these two sees both individuals and social institutions continually in need of God's grace because sin persists on both levels.

The preacher, then, seeks to speak at the corner of People Street and Power Street with a word to the baptized about their own and the world's need for liberating grace. If the baptized (who often live and work on Power Street) are to be responsible citizens, preachers must become especially attentive to these theological issues in periods around elections. This is not about using the pulpit to recommend certain candidates or parties. But the sermon could help the congregation to view politics as a vocation in which they have a part to play.[40]

The persistence of sin requires that we recognize our ongoing dependence on God's enabling Spirit.

Human Sin and Domestic Violence

The reality of sin and God's response of redemption imply the necessity for confession and repentance. This can be seen with particular poignancy by looking at the difficult subject of domestic violence, especially when it is present in the church. We need to allow ourselves to feel the depth of sin in such violence and not move simplistically to God's forgiveness of perpetrators. An impressive collection of essays and sermons, *Telling the Truth: Preaching about Sexual and Domestic Violence,*[41] confronts us with how close this issue is to congregations. This volume also refocuses our convictions about:

1. Violence and human defacement, divine suffering, and salvation;
2. God's compassion and God's wrath; and
3. Confession and repentance before forgiveness.

Violence and Human Defacement

Amid the pervasive presence of violence in North American society, preachers look out at congregations that include three kinds of people: victim-survivors, perpetrators, and bystanders. In the United States just under 15 percent of boys and more than 30 percent of girls are sexually molested before they are eighteen. More than three-quarters of the perpetrators are adults whom the children thought they could trust.[42] To think that some victim-survivors are not in the pews of the average congregation would be naïve. If this is so, it means that bystanders are likely present as well. It is also reasonable to assume we are also preaching to some abusers. Marie Fortune urges that in preaching we "must attempt to meet our pastoral and ethical responsibility to all three groups" and admits that is no easy task.[43]

The effect of violence is privation, whereas the evil of violence is its power to deface the human spirit. Thus, abuse victims characteristically view themselves as worthless and despicable, while abusers reduce persons to mere objects. Violence against women, says Wendy Farley, "is the excruciating transformation created when a person—an *imago Dei*—is treated as if she were a stone." Human sin has woven violence throughout the fabric of creation. This forces us, Farley argues, to begin theology not with assumptions of God's power, but "with the facticity of unjust suffering." Our understanding of salvation is that "it must make the soul capable of receiving its own beauty, and yet must do so in a way that ignites freedom rather than bypasses it."[44] This salvation is expressed in both compassion and wrath.

> *In the face of domestic violence, theology begins, not with God's power but with God's sorrow over unjust suffering.*

God's Compassion and Wrath

God is by nature compassionate. Compassion is the kind of power that redeems. "God created us for love out of love," and, therefore, suffering from sexual violation is contrary to God's intentions for human beings. Yet "suffering is one of the places where God is most intimately present." Preaching offers victims the compassionate presence of God. But, according to Farley, compassion for perpetrators takes the form of God's wrath. Rebuking violent people is compassionate work to enable them to recognize their need for transformation, without which forgiveness is impossible. Compassion's wrathful power may awaken both a feeling of the torture created by their own evil and a thirst for good.[45] Homiletically, we need to express God's righteous indignation against perpetrators and also against those who know what has been going on and have kept silent. Rebuke is sometimes a necessary sermonic form—one that can awaken a hearing and, hopefully, a sense of how God views the sin of domestic violence.

> *In the midst of domestic violence, compassion takes the form of wrath to rebuke those who are perpetrators.*

CONFESSION, REPENTANCE, AND FORGIVENESS

The church is prone to emphasize the gospel as a message of forgiveness. Applying this to domestic violence, the church's first reaction has been to encourage victim-survivors to forgive those who have abused and offended them. But this is a superficial interpretation of Jewish and Christian theological teaching. Both traditions emphasize that the responsibility for moving toward forgiveness rests with the offender, not the offended.

Only after the abuser has offered genuine confession and repentance can there be a context for real forgiveness and healing. Marie Fortune once spoke with a group of offenders. One of them advised her, "Whenever you talk with church leaders, tell them for us: don't forgive us so quickly." These offenders admitted that easy forgiveness "was the worst thing anyone could have done for them, because it meant that they could continue to avoid taking responsibility for the harm they had done."[46]

> *"Don't forgive us so quickly," says a sexual offender.*

Preaching to Sexual Abusers

John McClure explores how one should preach to perpetrators of sexual violence. He emphasizes that preachers should make sure the abusers know precisely the ugliness and hurt involved in their abusive actions. Only through such stark clarity can we hope to eliminate rationalization and self-deception. McClure also wants perpetrators to know that the violence done cannot be undone. He adds that this is not "the voice of judgment or condemnation."[47] But why avoid announcing God's anger against violence and those who violate others?

If our theology of forgiveness requires confession and repentance, clarity about the offense is only the first step. The grace of forgiveness is cheap unless it brings deep brokenness and mourning on the part of the sinner. Farley's comments on the compassionate work of wrath—noted above—indicate that restorative justice has its price and that the sermon should not back away from naming it. That price is more than a sense of guilt. It also involves seeing the pain the abuser has inflicted on the victim, on the victim's family and friends, and on God. Forgiveness becomes a reality only when the sinner realizes that the sinful act is ultimately not just an act against another person, but one against God. In making clear that God is angry with the evil of domestic violence, the key may be conveying the sense of pain and anguish that God suffers.[48]

In this chapter we have taken our theological convictions about God; human nature; and sin, repentance, and forgiveness to demonstrate their ethical import by connecting them with the practical issues of legalized gambling, genetic research, and domestic violence.

Homilectical Guidelines

Several matters need to be emphasized for the preacher.

1. The connection between theology and ethics need not always be made explicitly in a sermon.
2. Preachers contribute significantly to moral discernment simply by offering well-thought-out theology.
3. Yet more often than not, sermons need to clarify moral implications to enable congregations to make connections.
4. At other times, preachers will test their own theological assumptions and assertions by undertaking deliberate ethical reflection, even when no direct reference is to be made in the sermon itself.
5. After the sermon is prepared and before it is delivered, preachers can deliberate on its moral-theological dimension as a self-critical check. When both theology and ethical reflection have been reviewed with care, the sermon's images, stories, and descriptions as well as specific explanations and interpretations will reflect this engagement.

Having seen how three moral issues (gambling, genetic research, and domestic violence) intersect and challenge our basic beliefs, we see the importance of faith as the entry-point into preaching ethics.

We speak and listen as those who share the baptismal confession: Jesus Christ is Lord.

We now turn to the second area of our interconnected web, moral character. As people of faith, how are we and our community reflective of this faith? How do we embody ethics?

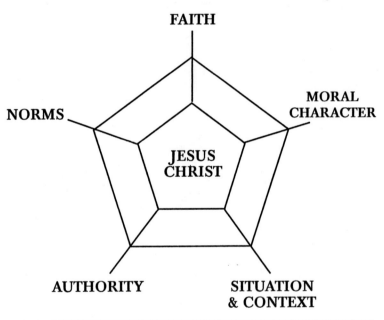

3

MORAL CHARACTER
Preaching Christian Discipleship

One way to understand preaching is to examine its role not just in inculcating a gospel perspective but also in forming moral character and enabling discipleship. In our last chapter we took the first step in ethical reflection when we explored how what we believe as Christians affects our approach to ethics. Now our second step invites exploration of how this faith is embodied in us both as individual Christians and as a community of Christians. We are seeking to answer the question, How does our character shape our approach to a specific moral issue? Ethicists name this "moral agency." Can preaching help congregations become a people who in their very persons express ethical integrity?[1]

We look first at how ethics is or needs to be incarnated. We start with the general issue of integrity and then move to a concrete ethical case drawn from the field of law. This leads us to reflect on professional ethics, a gospel understanding of moral character, and how we might communicate this to a congregation homiletically. The second stage of our exploration looks at the moral characteristics others see when they look at the church and when they encounter us as persons. We consider Paul's call to live by the Spirit rather than the flesh and examine what the church has traditionally named vices and virtues. As we come to greater clarity about the traits of character enabled by the gospel, we focus more directly on the preaching task.

Moral Character and Integrity

Politicians and other public figures often present themselves as people of "integrity," that is, people of moral character who can be trusted. When they betray such trust, we frequently criticize them as lacking ethical integrity. After the United States Supreme Court ruled on the Florida vote-count for president in the fall of 2000, much of the commentary in the public press debated whether or not the court had acted with integrity. What do we mean by integrity?

Stephen Carter, a Yale University law professor, wrote about the political virtues necessary for the survival of democracy. He argues that the first of these virtues is *integrity*.² Carter says he was inspired to pursue the theme of integrity by Dietrich Bonhoeffer's notion of discipleship as "unblinking obedience to God." Translated to the realm of public morality, this becomes "unblinking obedience to right."³

Carter goes on to spell out three fundamental elements that constitute integrity:

1. **discerning** right from wrong
2. **acting** on what is right, even at personal cost
3. **stating** openly that you are doing so

He admits that this runs counter to what we often experience. He remembers watching a televised football game in which a receiver caught a pass after it had touched the ground. This should have been ruled an incomplete pass, but the referee was not positioned to see the play accurately. The receiver reacted as though he had successfully caught the ball when he knew he had not. He hurried back to the huddle so that the next play could get underway before the previous one could be reviewed by video replay. Viewers like Carter, watching the play at home, saw the replay and, therefore, the deception. They also heard the play-by-play commentator commend the receiver's deceptive reaction as "a heads-up play." The truth, of course, is that this was a case of a player cheating and an announcer not only condoning but even commending cheating.

Carter muses about what might have happened if the receiver had gone to the referee and said, "No, I did not catch the ball before it hit the ground." The player's teammates, his coach, and many of the fans would likely have been furious with him. So he decided to play by the ethic of winning at all costs—an ethic that rewards cheating.⁴

How does the church enable its people to have a deep sense of what is right versus wrong, the courage to act on their convictions, and a boldness to declare this openly? At a very basic level the preacher seeks to call the congregation to a discipleship that puts integrity ahead of winning, whether on the playing field, in the market place, or at the ballot box. Integrity then is about seeking to integrate our lives with what Paul calls having the mind of Christ (1 Cor. 2:16). When this is seen for what it is, a countercultural stance, the sermon's contribution to the formation of Christian character may be recognized as more crucial and formidable than first suspected.

> *Preachers seek to call congregations to discipleship that puts integrity ahead of winning at all costs and links it to the mind of Christ.*

Moral Character and the Professions

We move now from the broad notion of integrity to the specific area of professional behavior. How does moral behavior in the area of the professions relate to moral character? A prominent Canadian legal case focuses this issue for us.

A Case of Legal Defense Ethics

In 1993 lawyer Ken Murray found himself defending Paul Bernardo, a notorious, terrifying serial rapist and murderer. For seventeen months before trial, Murray concealed videotapes of Bernardo's rape and torture of four teenage girls. Murray claimed that he was only doing this to undermine the prosecution's chief witness, Karla Homolka (Bernardo's wife at that time), who had clearly shared in these sadistic acts. It was, Murray argued, his duty to serve his client to the best of his ability–even though he found the videotapes (and the crimes they revealed) utterly revolting. Shortly before the case was to come to trial, Murray resigned as legal defense. The trial went forward with another lawyer who promptly exposed the existence of the tapes. As a result of Murray's concealment, Homolka received what many consider an astonishingly light plea-bargain sentence. Bernardo was still convicted and sentenced to life in prison. After the trial, Murray was charged with obstructing justice.

Murray's own case was then argued largely on a distinction between what the law allows (barely, at best) and his moral responsibility as a professional lawyer. Ontario Supreme Court Justice Patrick Gravely indicated that Murray had broken the law by withholding critical evidence from the police and the prosecution, but it was not clear that he had done so *intentionally*. At Murray's trial Austin Cooper, a leading defense lawyer, defended Murray. Cooper contended that Murray had a legal obligation not to turn the tapes over to the prosecutor because he was obligated to defend his client as best he could. The ruthless pragmatism of all this, Cooper acknowledged, is part of what lawyers do to get better deals for their clients. Ninety percent of cases are resolved by "wheeling and dealing, defending the indefensible, the daily cut-and-thrust of a lawyer's life." All of this, Cooper admitted, "sounds a little corrupt when one says it." He went on to argue that the tapes fall "into the grey zone, where there are no hard-and-fast rules."[5]

In an analysis of this case, criminal law professor Alan Young remarked that sometimes legal battles are waged at the expense of truth. The adversarial system, he acknowledged, is designed to seek not truth but fairness. It is inherently competitive and allows one's judgment to be skewed. "Winning at all costs becomes the measure of a lawyer's success." This value ought to be replaced by another, namely, "whether the lawyer participated in a process in which justice was served." He concluded, "Lawyers should receive training not only in advocacy but also with respect to their ethical obligations."[6] But such further education must transcend obligations or else lawyers may just learn more sophisticated ways to circumvent justice. What is needed is formation in the ethics of character–personal and professional.[7]

Lawyers have a primary obligation not to winning at all costs, but to serving the cause of justice.

The Larger Arena of Professional Ethics

Edward Pellegrino, director of the Georgetown Center for Medical Ethics, probes the need for *virtue ethics* in the professions and what this might look like in the area of medicine.[8] In so doing, he prepares us for the larger issue of the connection between moral character and ethical behavior.

Pellegrino notes that for two thousand years virtue as character formation was the major aim of ethics. Here, the emphasis was on what kind of persons we ought to be in general. For the professional person, this meant what kind of professional persons we are called to be. Aristotle spoke of excellence or virtue as that quality of character that makes persons good and enables them to do good things. Thomas Aquinas followed Aristotle when he spoke of dispositions necessary to perform good actions in accord with our end, or *telos,* as human beings.[9] This perspective has been eroded because our pluralistic, secular society cannot agree on what human nature is or on its purpose.

Kant saw virtue as obedience to duty, and Locke introduced the notion of personal rights that allows individuals to accept or deny any responsibilities that they may want. Virtue is even scorned by some because those without virtue can take advantage of those who try to live by it. In the marketplace, says Pellegrino, virtue can't compete.

Ethics requires character. We must eventually apply in daily life whatever principles we espouse in theory. But how does one know when and how to apply theoretical principles? Utilitarian calculation or weighing of consequences does not go far enough. We are thrown back to what we think or feel—which is ultimately based on what kind of persons we are. Virtue theory bridges the gap between knowing and doing. Why do some people habitually do what is right and good? Why do some people consistently treat others with respect or respond more appropriately to difficult life situations? The answers can be found only in their characters both as individuals and as professional people.

Each of the professions has a clearly defined goal or purpose. We can, for example, pair these:

- medicine and healing
- law and justice
- teaching and learning

Pellegrino focused especially on medicine. Because of the human predicament of illness, a person becomes a vulnerable, exploitable *patient*.[10] Patients have to trust their respective physicians to act in their best interests. The physician's knowledge is nonproprietary. Physicians covenant with society to use their knowledge for the good of society. This use of knowledge is dependent on their character and on their commitment to the good of others. The physician-patient relationship is promissory in keeping with the best interests of the patient (rather than the physician's own self-interest). Physicians are also members of what can be called a moral community—the medical profession. Because of this, they have a collective responsibility to be good stewards of medical knowledge for the benefit of society as a whole. In light of all this, Pellegrino concluded, the very nature of medicine requires physicians to have certain virtues both to be the kind of persons physicians need to be and to practice medicine well.[11]

Professional people need their professional associations to be moral communities reminding them of their ultimate calling.

THE GOSPEL AND MORAL CHARACTER

Pellegrino drew much of his argument from ancient Greek thought, particularly Aristotle. For the Greeks, a virtue was an excellence enabling a person to attain the highest potentialities of his or her nature. But the source of virtue for Christians is neither a learned skill nor an expression of human nature as such. For Christians, the source of virtue is a habit of the heart, a gift of the Spirit.[12] The contrast between a Christian understanding of virtue and one that is not Christian becomes even sharper when we look at the legacy of modernity and its way of distorting a Christian notion of freedom. Pellegrino helps Christian professionals ponder the question, How does our relationship to God shape our moral character and our behavior as professional persons?

Christians understand that moral character is rooted in a doctrine of human nature shaped by the life, death, and resurrection of Jesus Christ. We see our freedom and ourselves quite differently from that of Western society. Our freedom lies not in our choices but in our identity; we are free in Christ. "For freedom Christ has set us free" (Gal. 5:1). Our having certain intentions and convictions shapes our character. These make us who we are. Our character enables us to interact with what happens to us and to fit this into the larger narrative of God's story. We fit in not as we choose but as God calls. Our lives are simply a part of God's story.

For Christians, freedom lies not in our choices but in our identity; we are free in Christ.

The Enlightenment, Stanley Hauerwas points out, created the myth that we as individuals can make up our own minds about what is good or bad.[13] In our individualistic culture choice is everything, as though by choice we can shape our morality just as a shopper can select this over that in a grocery store. Our most defining characteristic then becomes our perpetual need to choose—and not just *what* to choose, but *that* we choose. Because this freedom to choose is centered in the individual, deception results. We deceive ourselves into thinking that our choices don't impinge on the choices of others and that theirs don't impinge on ours. Thus, secular society creates a philosophy of individualism in which the choosing *I* is central to existence.

The Christian response to individualism claims that the self needs to be de-centered.[14] The emphasis shifts from choosing to being called. Who we are *called to be* implies a caller, one who enables us to fulfill our calling. It is not all up to us. The narrative of our lives is not autobiography. It is a biography set in the larger context of history stretching back to creation and looking forward to new creation. The central actor is not us but God. His designation as our Creator makes us contingent, dependent persons. God is the chooser. We are the chosen.

The narrative of God's story is not just one-on-one with each individual. Rather, it is the story, as Hauerwas reminds us, of a people and a church. We read our lives within the communal journey of a fellowship of people. The members of this fellowship or congregation and the congregation as a whole shape our lives, form our identity, and help us navigate our moral way. *Virtue ethics*, as Hauerwas terms it, is communally contextual. That means it always develops and plays out in a specific context. The defining feature of that context is its nature as community rather than as individual. As Christians, we have a sense of our true purpose within a larger narrative that moves us beyond the imperative of merely individual choice.

> **Our identity as Christians is shaped by our communal journey within the larger narrative of God's long journey with Israel and the church.**

Our ultimate purpose is clarified in the life of ancient Israel, in the gospel accounts of the ministry of Jesus, and in the tradition of the church's seeking to live the life of Christ. Through this extended narrative our characters are formed as beings in the image of our Maker and Redeemer, and our view of the world around us is reshaped accordingly.[15]

Freedom, according to Hauerwas, is not derived from intellectual self-awareness but from acquired habits learned within our communal experience. We cannot, of course, guarantee freedom from determination because our freedom is connected to the adequacy and truthfulness of the descriptions we learn from the community within which we live. The lives of some people are much more determined by externalities than those of others. The Christian claim is that all of us have some capacity to respond to God's story. And that story frees us!

What is particularly striking in Hauerwas' analysis of freedom and moral character is his contention that we "acquire character through the expectation of others" who make us aware of our own restricted vision. So the community we choose to encounter (or be encountered by) becomes critically important for our character development. We do not create our own character; it is a gift from others. When we receive it as gift, it becomes ours. This means that my freedom is dependent on the trust I have in those who stand over against me. They clarify my *telos,* my calling.[16]

The traditions within which we live as Christians are not static and fixed. They are living, growing, and changing. It cannot be assumed that they lead only to good. Traditions can foster evil behavior and diminish moral rectitude. This is poignantly obvious in the church's traditions regarding the role and ministry of women. Our awareness that we are sinners drives us to keep on discerning the gospel's depiction of our freedom in Christ. Sin, as Reinhold Niebuhr reminds us, arises from insecurity that seeks to overcome through the will-to-power. We want to overreach our finitude and pretend that we are not limited creatures. Our religious rebellion against God leads to that moral will-to-power that subordinates others to ourselves and results in our injustice toward them.[17]

Preaching and Moral Character

As we turn to the homiletical influence on moral character, four observations may be helpful.

1. The preacher needs to **clarify the relationship between behavior and character,** make their connection explicit, and provide the necessary explanatory material to understand it. How was Ken Murray's behavior a reflection of his character? Would he have behaved differently if he had been shaped by the professional formation of character outlined by Pellegrino? It is hard to imagine that he wouldn't. In the accounting profession, the story of how Arthur Andersen's employees gradually developed a culture of greed, especially at senior management levels, is detailed in a chilling exposé by an ethics insider, Barbara Toffler, in *Final Accounting: Ambition, Greed, and the Fall of Arthur Andersen.*[18]

2. The preacher needs to **tell the story**–simplified sufficiently to be accessible–so that the whole congregation shares at least some limited version. The Murray story, appearing as it did in the news media over a long period of time, became extremely complex. Just alluding to it in a sermon as though everyone knows it is too presumptuous because some may have missed certain parts of it or may have read or heard quite a different version than others have. Also, newspapers and television stations often slant their coverage on many controversial topics. The preacher must give as straightforward an account of the story as possible. Through this shared rehearsal, the preacher helps the congregation experience the

story in that moment in the sermon. Narrative experience is integral to the formation of character.

3. The preacher needs to **grapple extensively with the way Christian character is distinctively formed** in contrast to secular assumptions about human freedom and personal identity. Spelling out some of this in a given sermon can lend clarity and vividness. Explanation and interpretation help congregations think through basic assumptions about character formation.

4. The preacher must recognize that the **character-forming role of preaching may happen subtly over time.** Months and even years of preaching develop in the congregation a gradual awareness of what it means to live with integrity and to act out of commitment to goals such as caring for others and upholding a just social order. Sometimes we come to insight with a more sudden and surprising experience of faith, as in the case of two followers of Jesus on Easter Sunday afternoon (Luke 24). Will Willimon sermonically probes their difficulty in recognizing Jesus until he "broke bread" in their home. Modern people, he says, think that they can see beyond their predecessors as though the only valid way of seeing is scientific or psychological. Spiritual seeing is excluded as though the world is closed to receiving messages from beyond. The two Emmaus travelers were locked into their own little world and needed the risen Christ to invite them and enable them to see beyond their limited horizons. The gospel invites us, says Willimon, to be open to messages that are not self-derived, indeed to be willing to have our lives commandeered by something other than our own egos need. At the baptism of Jesus the heavens *were ripped in two* (the Greek word here is particularly vivid). This is not just a metaphorical way of saying that we can now get to God because the heavens are open and the Spirit has descended. Rather, because of Jesus, the heavens are ripped open, and now God can get to us![19]

The character-forming role of preaching may happen subtly over time after months or even years, or in a sudden seeing of reality through the gospel.

As Jesus challenged the Emmaus pair and exploded their limited perspectives of Easter day, the preacher clarifies how the gospel stands over against the congregation to enable them to feel the powerful pull of a force from beyond themselves. Part of the problem preachers sometimes have, according to Willimon, is that their desire to be well thought of interferes with their calling to help clarify the truth of the gospel. He tells the story of a student on the Duke University campus who had never been to chapel and had no intention of going. When, as dean of the chapel, Willimon asked why, the student said that at that time things were going well in his life and he didn't want to get "jerked around" by God as a result of going to worship in the chapel. Maybe, Willimon muses, we should put up a warning sign at the chapel entrance: "Please don't risk coming in here if you don't want to be jerked up by the collar and moved to somewhere where you haven't been before." This is not so different from the apostle Paul's assertion, "Don't let the world squeeze you into its own mold but let God remold your minds from within" (Rom. 12:2, J. B. Phillips).

Preaching can lead the congregation to transformed character because the gospel is invitation. It is God's love in Christ that transforms. The word of grace has always been more transforming than the word of judgment. The preacher who is prophetically effective in communicating the newness and distinctiveness of the word of God is the one who speaks with the compassion of a pastor. Like the physician who has to tell the patient the truth, the pastor feels the deep pain, even sorrow, that the truth can bring.

The Characteristics of Moral Character | individual

General terms can carry us only so far in describing how our relationship before God is reflected in what we do. We manifest our characters by attitudes and specific characteristics. Others see what our character is through the posture we take toward life and the dispositions or qualities that we reveal in our actions.

Our convictions about who we are as God's people mold our stance toward life. Our lives are communally framed, and our journeys are woven into the fabric of God's journey with our planet and human history. We are not the masters of our fate or the creators of our destiny. We are individuals called to live in community in *God's* world. We are not ultimately fearful or cynical, because the story of life is finally *God's* story. Yes, like the psalmists, we have many questions, many complaints, many imponderables; but in the end, the root metaphor of the psalms is "the LORD reigns."[20] This metaphor provides us with a posture toward life that we can finally express only in doxology. Anderson reminds us that in "Jesus Christ we see the character of the mysterious God the creator," and in the Holy Spirit we taste God's transforming power. This is a stance of doxology that "generates confidence and openness in a troubled world with the knowledge that the very real powers of evil are not the final word."[21]

When Nelson Mandela emerged in 1990 from twenty-six years of darkness in the Robben Island and Pollsmoor prisons, his spirit was filled with light. The depth of his faith became evident to the world as he radiated a posture of uncommon grace.[22]

> *Our characters are rooted in the character God revealed in Jesus Christ, and in the Spirit we are transformed to be able to live as God's people.*

Character Traits—Virtues and Vices

Who we are is seen through our persistent tendencies and operative habits. These have been called *virtues* if they are viewed as positive and *vices* if they are seen as negative.[23] The letters of various writers (especially Paul) to the early church are quite specific about what are regarded as virtues and vices in light of the gospel. In Galatians 5,[24] Paul urged the congregations in the Roman province of Galatia to live by the Spirit rather than by what he calls "the flesh." To live according to the flesh is not a contrast between what is natural and what is spiritual. Rather, it refers to living as though we can live in our own strength and don't need God.[25] To ignore God in this way is to deny our creaturehood and oppose God's creatorship.

VICES TO RESIST

Paul, therefore, listed vices that Christians are to resist. If we are "led by the Spirit," we are not subject to the power that lies behind these behaviors. This power of evil denies the freedom we have in Christ and distorts human nature (in terms of sexuality and health) and human relationships.

Preachers may feel reluctant to preach on one or more of these vices. They may not want to be seen telling others how to behave. They may simply join modern culture in dismissing such vices as outdated teachings no longer taken seriously. When preachers allow themselves to be guided by Paul's approach here, they will note that the apostle did not begin with behavior. Instead, he began with our characters under the influence of the Spirit, our freedom in Christ to transcend temptation. He avoided the moralism of telling people to change their lives by their own efforts. Rather, he pointed them to God's transforming grace that enables moral character. Such grace is discerned when the sermon indicates explicitly that we are enabled to live our discipleship by the energy of the Spirit of Jesus Christ.

Character that exemplifies Christian virtues is enabled by God's transforming grace in Jesus Christ.

Church tradition identifies "seven deadly sins": pride, envy, anger, sloth, greed, gluttony, and lust. Particularly noteworthy for us is how society in Western culture has tended to minimize, twist, or even reverse some of these vices that for almost two millennia have been regarded as negative. Advertisers regularly appeal to lust, envy, and even a bit of gluttony. Pride has become ambiguous because taking pride in oneself and asserting one's own agenda are frequently praised, even though other forms of self-assertion may still be criticized. As for greed, it has actually been promoted positively in a television program by that very name! When our secular culture makes God irrelevant for all practical purposes, we should not be surprised that people today, even people in our congregations, ignore the destructiveness of these vices. Nor should we be surprised that larger or smaller groups of people, including congregations sometimes, manifest behavior that distorts and undermines constructive and healthy relationships. So Paul urged the congregation in Philippi to be of a common mind and to show generous regard for one another rather than act selfishly and out of self-interest. He invited them—and us—to have the mind of Christ (Phil. 2:1–5).

VIRTUES TO INCARNATE

Returning to Paul's list of virtues, we note that this is not a series of individual character traits from which we choose one or more. Paul calls them "fruits of the Spirit." They are not imperatives, nor are they "spiritual gifts" (in the sense of 1 Cor. 12), as though this virtue is given to one person and that one is given to another. Rather, the list forms a self-contained unit. Those who live by the Spirit have a capacity for love, joy, peace, patience, kindness, generosity, faithfulness, gentleness, and self-control. All these qualities of character flow from the person of Christ.

The church lives by this set of virtues as a whole. It is peaceable so the world can see that church members are a people who hope for God's kingdom. It manifests love because this is required to sustain relationships. Patience is needed in a violent world marked by so much injustice, because we have to wait on God's promised kingdom of *shalom* (peace with justice). Yes, we plan and implement justice and peace programs, but we act in light of how we see the end of the story as God's ending. While God may use us to help create some part of *shalom,* our task lies in being faithful to these virtues that witness to the reality of the Spirit in the life of the church.[26] This set of virtues is both shared by the whole community and available for each Christian.

> *The virtues that flow from the gospel are available to both individual Christians and the Christian community as a whole.*

One of the underused resources for discerning the formation of moral character is the biblical wisdom tradition. In some ways it corresponds to our society's search for character. But as Alyce McKenzie points out, it does so in ways very different from what our culture expects.[27] Biblical wisdom is a body of admonitions (imperatives) and proverbs (indicative sayings) communally shared as part of a lifelong process of learning. It explicates relationships between members of the community and between the community and God. Wisdom is neither a human accomplishment nor a matter of self-fulfillment. It is a gift from God through Christ that enables faithfulness to God in good times and bad. For concrete examples of wisdom preaching, see McKenzie's compelling sermons in *Preaching Proverbs.*[28]

Preaching and Communal Moral Character

Preaching includes reawakening the congregation's moral character and summoning listeners in the name of the gospel to the moral imperative to be Christ's disciples, individually and collectively. How may this happen in a sermon?

It may sound presumptuous to assume that the moral character of Christians and the Christian community needs awakening. The need for awakening becomes obvious when we recall that we are continually being socialized in an alien culture. Many scholars and preachers recognize a steady and disturbing decline in societal standards. This decline reflects a weakening sense of vice in our individual and collective moral character. This becomes even more obvious in light of the increasing level of tolerance for violence; a distorted patriotism that supports preemptive military strikes against other countries; lust in television programming, popular movies, novels, and video games; and shameless greed in business practices.[29] Some preachers are bolder than others in drawing this decline to the church's attention.[30]

Here, we note four ways in which preaching can deliberately call the church to be a community of moral character:

1. Concretizing theology and character formation through story—a theme already noted but worth repeating. Christian character can be clarified when preaching connects Christian theology with behavior. Brian Gerrish retells J. B. Priestley's play "An Inspector Calls" in which members of a well-to-do English family are gathered for an engagement party. A police inspector interrupts the party to report that a young woman has just committed suicide. It turns out that the young woman had encountered each of these "nice family people," and all had shown her the dark side of their respective characters. One or another demonstrated greed, anger, lust, drunkenness, and a disregard for truth. Their actions are described, not named abstractly. No one admits responsibility for creating the despair that finally lead to suicide. We, too, says Gerrish, "shrug off our trivial lapses from grace as though they could not possibly matter." He then explains that *original sin* "means that we are all tangled up together in sin" and that God holds us guilty "because our sins have caused others to fall." The blood of this young woman, like the blood of Abel, cries out in judgment. Yet the final word is a word of grace: The blood of Christ purifies our conscience to serve the living God![31]

Too often we "shrug off our trivial lapses from grace as though they could not possibly matter."

The character-changing power of the gospel enables us to unveil the presence of evil within us. The use of such a story and the careful nuancing of interpretation awaken both the imagination (through story—drawing the congregation in at a "heart" level) and the intellect (giving interpretation to deepen theological understanding). What is finally transforming is not guilt but grace. Grace, however, requires that the need for transformation be felt. To do so, we may have to admonish listeners outside our stories as Jesus the storyteller par excellence was prepared to do time and again.

2. Inspiring through example. A second way of calling the congregation to explore character is through the use of inspiring examples. The affirmation of virtues such as love, hope, patience, and compassion frequently takes the form of stories of exemplary figures such as Archbishop Oscar Romero, the Salvadorian martyr; Jean Vanier, the international humanitarian; and Kim Phuc, the Vietnamese war survivor. Sometimes a lesser-known person such as Dr. Michelle Brill-Edwards, a senior civil bureaucrat, is thrust into the news for daring actions such as speaking out against substandard practices and thus exposing a government "culture of deceit."

Dr. Brill-Edwards quit her high-profile job and founded the Alliance for Public Accountability. A colleague calls her "one of those rare individuals who come into your life and leave an indelible mark. A more honest soul I've never seen. She oozes integrity."[32] Such illustrations can be helpful because they incarnate virtues that Christians should manifest. But the exemplary approach can easily become moralistic. Moralistic preaching happens when we state or imply that we can change ourselves rather than be changed by God. Preaching moves beyond moralism by demonstrating how the virtues are expressions of the Spirit and are made possible through the gospel of Christ.[33] We do not and cannot create these qualities of character. Paul urged the Galatian church to "walk by the Spirit." His imperative leads directly to an emphatic future negative: "Then you will never gratify the desires of the flesh" (Gal. 5:16, author's translation). This is gospel rather than law.[34]

> *Moralistic preaching happens when we state or imply that we can change ourselves rather than be changed by God.*

3. Naming sin with boldness. Congregations, including many people in business, yearn to hear a word that will help them grapple with the reality of wrongdoing and evil in their world. Sermons can explain both what sin is and what is sin. The preacher can then demonstrate how sin emerges in society in very specific ways.

Ted Peters explores the path toward radical evil beginning with the fear of loss and the failure to trust. This leads to making the self number One and lusting after what other people have. Scapegoating others and enjoying another's suffering follows. Finally, evil manifests itself directly against God and becomes the destruction of the inner soul.[35] Sermons that unmask this reality by using exposition, vivid stories, and images provide insight and open listeners to rediscover the cross as the place where ultimate evil is finally confronted.

> *People in various areas of their lives yearn to hear a word that will help them grapple with the reality of wrongdoing and evil.*

4. Bringing insight through gospel connection. We look, finally, at how a very moving story can reach beyond our admiration to give us insight when it is connected with the gospel.

Gracia Grindal tells the true story of a surgeon who had to operate on a young woman for a cancerous growth on her cheek. This required cutting the nerve that controlled the muscles of her mouth. After the operation the patient looked at her misshapen mouth in a mirror and asked the surgeon if it would always look that way. He admitted that it would. She began to cry until her young husband knelt beside her and said, "I like it." Then he shaped his mouth to hers and kissed her. The surgeon looking on felt, he said, as though he was in the presence of God. The preacher then added, "So it is for us: God, in Christ, has come to us, conformed himself to our lives so we might be transformed."[36]

The story becomes a metaphor, and Christ becomes incarnate in the sermon. This forms the basis on which the congregation can be called to be who, by grace, they are. When they become who they are, the congregation manifests the fruits of the Spirit and exercises a significant formative influence on its individual members.

Stories can become metaphors through which Christ can become incarnate in the sermon.

In this chapter we have explored ethical aspects of moral character. We have sought to answer the question, How does our character shape our approach to a given issue? We have concluded that who we are is a reflection of what we believe. Through the lens of professional behavior, we clarified just how central being moral persons is to acting with moral integrity. We then looked more explicitly at the attitudes and character traits that ought to be true of us if we are disciples of Jesus Christ. We made the connection between ourselves as individual Christians and the community of the church. Within the context of the church our proclamation of the gospel has the power to inspire and form us as moral persons and as a moral community. This prepares us for discerning how the gospel calls us to act. For this we need the guidance of norms, values, and rights, to which we now turn.

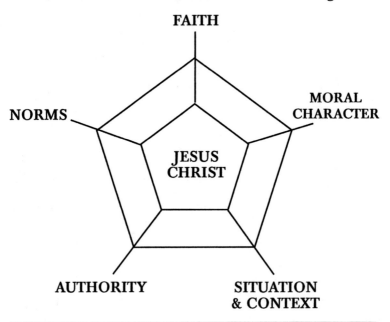

4

NORMS

Preaching That Clarifies Gospel Requirements

What are our obligations as God's people? We preach to the baptized. We assume our listeners are people of faith and are committed to being a community of disciples. But what requirements does the gospel place on its adherents? How is our relationship before God reflected in what we are doing? This is the third area of our ethical web.

Jazz improvisation, Bill Evans explains, is like a form of Japanese visual art in which the artist "must paint on a thin stretched parchment with a special brush and black water paint." It is an exceedingly delicate process: Any "unnatural or interrupted stroke will destroy the line or break through the parchment." No changes or amendments are possible. Artists must discipline themselves so that the idea in their heads is transmitted to their hands so directly that no deliberation can interfere. The resulting production may lack the complexity and textures of ordinary painting, but it does capture something that defies explanation. So with jazz improvisation, "direct deed is the most meaningful reflection."[1]

Preaching seeks to inculcate an approach to ethics where the deed proceeds straight from the heart without calculation. Moral acts cannot be separated from who we are in Christ. We are not just following the rules but expressing the gospel that has shaped us. Will Campbell calls this "abiding in grace" rather than "abiding by law."[2] We seek discipleship, not moralism. The gospel enables the former; the latter stresses our own efforts. Still, the gospel issues moral imperatives. Thus, we seek clarity about various kinds of norms that express our faith and commitments.

> *Preaching seeks to inculcate an approach to ethics where the deed proceeds straight from the heart without calculation.*

Norms and Definitions

In general, norms are standards by which we assess who we are and what we do. Obligations (often spelled out in rules) are norms that specifically indicate what are right actions without qualification. Micah responded to the rhetorical question, "What does the LORD require of you / but to do justice, and to love kindness, / and to walk humbly with your God?" (Mic. 6:8). Principles are norms that outline general directions for behavior, as in "love your neighbor as yourself." Values (or what we believe is "the good") are norms that clarify desired outcomes or consequences. The values of friendship and good health guide behavior with regard to human relationships or health care respectively. Rights (such as freedom or adequate necessities to sustain life) are claims that individuals or groups make on society.[3]

These are all connected under the rubric of norms because they clarify how we are called to live our lives. We will deal with each of them in turn:

1. We begin with norms as obligations and look at our most familiar statements of obligation: the Decalogue and the Sermon on the Mount.

2. We move to the normative principles of love-of-neighbor (explored concretely with reference to the issue of euthanasia) and justice.[4]

3. We focus on certain values, both personal and corporate (particularly in business), and ways in which these might be expressed in a sermon.

4. We probe contemporary interest in human rights and how preaching on them might strengthen discipleship.

The Ethics of Obligation

Our secular culture often ignores or rejects obligations. The popular Beatles song "All You Need Is Love" illustrates the permissive, self-help worldview that rejects any notion of others' laying expectations on us. The world of business constantly pressures governments to reduce "red tape" or leave it up to corporations to regulate themselves. A publication on corporate ethics recently printed an editorial entitled "Forget Compliance, Think Governance." To be sure, as the editorial points out, a narrow focus on not running afoul of the law is inadequate. Thus, strengthening the role and ability of board members would be a positive development. But the Enron/WorldCom fiascos only emphasize more strongly corporate society's moral failures under the impetus of deregulation and the refusal to understand a positive role for laws that protect the common good. Many argue that such laws would diminish competitiveness. This is unconvincing given the large numbers of participants involved in corporate shenanigans resulting in stockholder losses calculated in the trillions of dollars.[5] Our understanding of sin as both personal and systemic challenges idealistic notions about self-regulation, whereas our view of the pervasiveness of the work of God's Spirit keeps us from despair and encourages hope. We do not place such hope in human systems per se but in the possibility that establishing norms can enable accountability.[6]

COUNTERCULTURAL NORMS

Sermons, therefore, that begin with God's requirements, imperatives for discipleship, and taking up the cross are distinctly out of sync with our society. Yet they often reflect the thrust of biblical passages. Jesus spoke about a new commandment, "Love one another...as I have loved you" (Jn. 13:34), and called for a radical kind of discipleship, "deny [yourself] and take up [your] cross daily and follow me" (Lk. 9:23). Paul urged bearing "one another's burdens, and...fulfill the law of Christ" (Gal. 6:2). Some of this is particularly odd to Western ears: the command to love, the law of Christ. We expect an invitation to love and the gospel of Christ; instead, we get the language of obligation.[7] Preachers might sensitize their listeners to ethics if they made this countercultural direction clear at the beginning of the sermon.

> *Sermons that begin with God's requirements are distinctly out of sync with our society, yet often reflect the thrust of biblical passages.*

The question is not just about diminished standards. The larger issue becomes, Who sets the standards and why? Within the framework of our faith we do not begin with ourselves (or our self-interest). Faith begins with God who created us, loves us, and by grace forgives us. So over and over the Bible articulates moral demands. They are grounded in our transcendent existence as creatures made and redeemed in God's image. Our obligations are related to our recognition that we are in God's world, called to serve God's purposes.[8]

This transcendent God calls us to "impossible possibilities," as Niebuhr put it, by enabling our obedience through Christ. For this, of course, we need faith to see both that "life is good in spite of evil and evil in spite of good." We connect our lives to the One who is before us as Creator and after us as Judge, who is with us as Savior on the cross of Christ. The crucified one reveals "not only the possibilities but also the limits of human finitude in order that a more ultimate hope may arise from the contrite recognition of those limits."[9]

Congregations want guidance in how to orient their lives to the transcendent purposes of God for all of life. So the preacher helps the congregation to acquire "the intellectual confidence to question the standard way of doing business,"[10] whether in the world of work or the exercise of the professions or the arenas of family or politics. The sermon can show them how to affirm life while critically engaging the powers of evil. This theological framework brings us to the need for normative statements, as in the Ten Commandments and the Sermon on the Mount. They spell out what God's way of obedience entails.

THE TEN COMMANDMENTS AS NORMS TO SPELL OUT COVENANT OBLIGATIONS

God chose Israel as "my people" and entered into a covenant relationship with them (Ex. 19–20; 24). Next, God chose a means of defining and clarifying that relationship so that Israel would know what it meant to be God's covenantal partner. The "thou shalt not" statements of the Decalogue must be read as expressions of God's covenant with a people brought out of slavery in Egypt and given a new beginning as God's holy nation. Law is imbedded in the Torah story; these injunctions flow out of the narrative of God's journey with Israel.[11]

According to John Calvin, the Decalogue has three uses:

1. The law helps us see the character of a holy and loving God and our own finitude and sinfulness.
2. It awakens in us a fear of the consequences of not following God's ways for us.
3. It instructs the believing community on how to live the will of God by the power of the Spirit.[12]

The first three commandments (Ex. 20:1–7; Deut. 5:6–11) confess who God is. God is redeemer and totally preeminent. This means no rivals, no props that could become substitutes for God, and no use of God's name that attempts to manipulate God. Discipleship begins with a deep respect for who God is and loyalty to this saving One. It begins without any misrepresentations of God or misuse of God's name. These are summarized in the first great commandment: "You shall love the LORD your God with all your heart, and with all your soul, and with all your might" (Deut. 6:5; cf. Mk. 12:30).

The second section of the Law (Ex. 20:8–17; Deut. 5:12–21) orders the lives of individuals in community to express covenantal identity. Their relationship with God is to be mirrored in their relationships to one another through their observance of the Sabbath, honoring parents, and respect for the person and property of others. All spheres of life are touched on in principle: the individual, the family, the legal system, the marketplace, and, by implication, the political realm. The restrictions are all meant to ensure *shalom,* the health and harmony that allows the whole community to experience God's covenantal blessing.[13]

> *The first three of the Ten Commandments confess who God is as covenantal partner; the last seven order the lives of individuals in community to express covenantal identity.*

These broad general principles in the Decalogue are applied to various aspects of Israel's life through case law developed over many centuries. Two primary, imaginative traditions enabled Israel to discern what it means to continue the obedience called for at Sinai. One is the command tradition of Deuteronomy, which has been described as "preached law." This interpreted the Law for new situations. The other is the instruction tradition of Leviticus and other priestly writings in Exodus and Numbers. This gave guidance as to how Israel was to live with the inscrutable mystery of God's presence in an alien world. The Decalogue principles remain clear, but their expression in life requires ongoing creative discernment.[14]

> *The goal of preaching is to translate rules into guiding norms shaped by a gospel perspective.*

In a Lenten sermon, "The Rules of the Freedom Game," Fleming Rutledge contrasts a "teeth-grittin' Christianity" that is never sure it is good enough with a free and joyous game based on gospel. Within the family of God, the Ten Commandments reflect and solidify identity and belonging. Rutledge gives a simple illustration of standing in a pharmacy. Suddenly she realized that stealing was just not something she would do. Why? Because of who she understood herself to be as a member of a certain Virginia family. This sudden recognition had nothing to do with a prohibition but everything to do with who she is. This means that she doesn't have to go through any mental gymnastics about calculating the risks of getting caught. She is free. This is freedom from and also freedom for. The commandments are not isolated in some segregated part of life. They have been integrated into the whole of life as a part of personal and corporate identity.

For the individual and the congregation, God's goodness takes shape in life's constant daily struggle. In this struggle we must have the guidance of principles such as the Ten Commandments. Seen this way, they are loving commandments. Embracing them gives liberty and fosters growth.[15] But we only recognize these normative statements as loving commandments when we internalize them into our character as a gift of grace.

Here we see our ethical web in full play, for homiletically the ethics of obligation (norms) has been integrated with the ethics of faith and of character in the situational context of daily living under the authority of scripture. The commandments are imbedded in the story of redemption and therefore are also read from the perspective of freedom in Christ. The prejudices against taking this set of rules seriously are lifted and its alternative–loving obedience–is concretely presented. This gospel approach to the Law reminds us of who we are called (and freed) to be.[16]

THE SERMON ON THE MOUNT AS A PROCLAMATION OF OBLIGATION

The requirements for discipleship in the New Testament go beyond the Decalogue and its implied social order. The Sermon on the Mount (Mt. 5–7) begins with beatitudes, not commands. They are poetic promises that reflect God's alternative order. People who are poor, who mourn, who are meek and hungry, for example, are blessed in the kingdom Jesus inaugurated. Old prohibitions are extended: Don't kill becomes don't be angry; don't commit adultery becomes don't lust. Rules regarding divorce and making oaths are made more stringent. Expectations keep on getting tougher: Turn the other cheek; love your enemies. None of this makes any sense—unless these are descriptions of the world as it will be in the fullness of time and of which we are already participants through Christ. Because we know our destination and the harmony and joy that will be, we look at these as the ethic of our ultimate identity. Only this allows us to appreciate the supreme challenge, "Be perfect, therefore, as your heavenly Father is perfect" (Mt. 5:48).

> *The Sermon on the Mount doesn't make sense—unless it is a description of the world as it will be in the fullness of time and of which we are already participants through Christ.*

Jesus' masterful Sermon on the Mount thus gives both overarching principles and specific rules. It is not enough for preachers to draw out principles and leave behind the specifics. These specific requirements drive us to realize that living up to Christ's expectations is impossible without God. But with God, these expectations become a powerful perspective that exposes the fragility of all human constructs and explodes the imagination toward vibrant possibilities.[17]

Preaching on the Decalogue or the Sermon on the Mount requires relating them respectively to the redemptive narrative of Sinai and the reign of God. The ethic of a new order calls for seeing others as God sees them and loving them with God's love. Again, there is no genuine obedience without communion with God.[18] The Sermon on the Mount spells out the ethics of obligation, but as a joyous journey of faith with Christ. Some years ago at a meeting of the Academy of Homiletics, Fred Craddock preached a sermon on the vision of the new Jerusalem in Revelation 22. He pictured the scene in vivid detail, and as he did so, the reality of God's alternative order struck me with fresh force. When the sermon renders God's new order visible, congregations are pulled to live out Christian discipleship and are open to hearing the injunctions of the Sermon on the Mount. A caveat, however, is in order here. Will Willimon reminds us that calling congregations to follow these chapters in Matthew 5–7 and take seriously injunctions such as loving our enemies does not make sense in our world and needs to be grounded theologically. We are to love like this because God loves like this.[19]

NORMATIVE PRINCIPLES: LOVE AND JUSTICE

From the obligations embodied in the Ten Commandments and the Sermon on the Mount, we turn to the normative principles of love and justice. Ethicists often regard the double command to love God totally and our neighbor as ourselves (Mk. 12:29–31) as the most fundamental principle of ethics. In a sense the Beatles were right. All we need is love. But this love is rooted in grace rather than attraction, or even gratitude. It is love of God for God's own sake and love of our neighbor for our neighbor's sake. This love even transcends family loyalties. This is a liberating love in a way diametrically opposed to our culture's notion of freedom.

> *Many ethicists regard the double command to love God totally and our neighbor as ourselves as the most fundamental principle of ethics.*

The command to love and the law of Christ focus our need for a different freedom, a freedom needed because of human sinfulness. We cannot of ourselves be altruistic. We cannot act out of love as an exercise of will. Why? Because our self-concern is too great. Sin is woven into the very fabric of human nature, creating an estrangement from God and our neighbor.[20] God's grace frees us to love. Yes, through divine grace we can be urged, even commanded, to love. Duty becomes delight in the dialectic of the profoundly unconditional love of God and the massively conditional need of human sinfulness.[21] As long as preaching maintains this dialectic of unconditional love and human sinfulness, it avoids legalism on the one hand and cheap grace on the other.

THE NORMATIVE PRINCIPLE OF LOVE-OF-NEIGHBOR AND THE MORAL QUESTION OF MERCY KILLING

In this chapter the overarching question of norms remains: How is our relationship before God reflected in what we are doing? Again, focusing on a specific issue can help us discover an answer. So we will probe the ethical implications of the principle of love of neighbor and relate them to a specific moral case. The case we have chosen is the mercy killing of Tracy Latimer, which made Canadian newspaper headlines over a period of several years. In this way we seek to explicate what it really means to love our neighbor as a corollary of loving God. Adding "as a corollary of loving God" reminds us that only as we stand with our neighbor as equals before the unequaled God can we truly love our neighbor as ourselves.

Tracy, age twelve, suffered from a severe form of cerebral palsy. She could not walk, talk, or care for herself, but she knew how to laugh and to love. She faced tough surgery to relieve painful tension in her muscles. One day in 1993 her father Robert Latimer took her to his car and asphyxiated her by means of carbon monoxide poisoning. Was this an act of love of neighbor? Robert Latimer claims that he only killed his daughter out of deep compassion. Her persistent pain had defined her life, and he acted to relieve her suffering. He believed euthanasia, "good death" or mercy killing, was better than life.

Latimer's action opened a tremendous debate. A jury of his peers convicted him of second-degree murder. The jury—with the concurrence of the trial judge—believed he should receive a reduced sentence of one year (instead of the legally required minimum of ten). The court's decision was appealed all the way to the Supreme Court. The highest court unanimously agreed that he had committed second-degree murder and sentenced him to the required minimum sentence. This was not, they added, cruel and unusual punishment.

This case has international implications because mercy killing can happen anywhere. Two issues, among many, can be noted. The more general one has to do with euthanasia as an act of mercy and love. Within this stands the specific issue of whether the minimum sentence is fair, given that others who commit murder in acts of violence and rage often receive the same minimum sentence. These two issues are intertwined in this case just as love of neighbor and concerns about justice are inevitably connected.

In regards to euthanasia, the Supreme Court of Canada stated, "Killing a person—in order to reduce suffering by a medically manageable physical or mental condition—is not a proportionate response to the harm represented by the non-life-threatening suffering from that condition." The Court acknowledged that Latimer "faced challenges that most Canadians can only imagine. His care of his daughter for many years is admirable. His decision to end his daughter's life is an error of judgment." The justices took the unusual step of indicating that an appeal could be made to the government to offer clemency. Latimer's defense lawyer commented afterwards that his client "may be legally guilty but in his heart of hearts he knows that what he did was morally what he had to do."[22] That comment puts this case squarely in the arena of ethics.

Ethicist Arthur Schaffer disagrees with the Supreme Court's sentence ruling. He argues that it confuses categories. Many people have seen the Court uphold the rights of the disabled. They therefore feel that their rights have been upheld in this decision because the sentence is the same as for any other person. But Schaffer notes that the original jury concluded "that Latimer did not kill his daughter because of her disability" but "because of his belief that she was in continual, acute, and unrelievable pain; and they empathized with the tragic situation in which the family found itself." Did Latimer receive his due when he was sentenced? Schaffer contends that compared with other murderers and compared with other countries that differentiate between killing out of mercy and killing out of hate or anger, he did not.[23] We will return to our discussion of justice below, but let us first turn to the moral question of euthanasia.

Currently, in discussions of euthanasia much of the language of obligation has been changed to the language of rights, as in the "right-to-die movement."

What complicates any current discussion of euthanasia is the changing attitude in society regarding this subject. The language of obligation has been changed to the language of rights, as in the "right-to-die movement" (in Oregon and The Netherlands particularly). Turning this issue into a matter of rights is a reflection of a cultural evolution in progress since the Enlightenment.[24] It is ironic that an increased acceptance of euthanasia should emerge at the point in Western societies where the availability of palliative care has progressed significantly and where the financial resources are sufficient to alleviate so much suffering. But this is also a time when such resources are not being made readily available. As a result, people fear being left helpless and dependent on technology. The cost is also out of reach for people in the U.S. dependent on Medicaid. Even private insurance companies often do not cover certain home-care or hospice expenses. As a result, impoverishing costs become crushing burdens for the families of the dying.

Beyond these important considerations, the deeper question has to do with God's presence in our living and in our dying and also with our living beyond our dying. Earlier, we affirmed that in life and in death we belong body and soul to Jesus Christ. We do not face death without hope or without God's suffering compassion. Our neighbor also belongs equally to God. We have given up the right to control our own destiny and also any right to determine the destiny of others. This is the perspective largely missing in our culture, as shown in the moving PBS series "On Our Own Terms: [Bill] Moyers On Dying."[25]

The discussions in the press about the fate of Tracy Latimer, whose life did not belong to her father but to God, also miss this transcendent viewpoint. Such a perspective does not mean that parents do not struggle. It does, however, mean that the church is the kind of community that can surround the Tracys of this world and their parents with the sustaining love of Christ. Jean Vanier is one who has demonstrated this love of neighbor as few others. His network of L'Arche homes for the acutely mentally and physically disabled witnesses to transcendent love.[26] Suffering is, finally, a spiritual condition and requires a spiritual response. The law of love calls the church through its preaching to probe these issues with sensitivity and persistence and to bear witness for the dying to the triumph of life.[27]

THE NORMATIVE PRINCIPLE OF JUSTICE—THE ENACTMENT OF LOVE

The connection between the principle of love-of-neighbor and justice is implied in a Christian reading of justice. Beginning with love of neighbor focuses our attention more sharply on the radicality of justice in preaching—radicalness in the sense of both deep-rooted and cultural over-against-ness. In Western society, justice commonly means something punitive and is based not on love but fear. The primary purpose of punitive justice appears to be retribution. Calls for justice usually imply stricter laws with larger penalties (especially, longer periods of incarceration), less attention to parole, putting people into bureaucratic categories, victim impact statements to influence sentencing, and more frequent and more rapid execution of people on death row. In the aftermath of the terrorist attacks on the U.S., some (no doubt in their rage and sorrow) called for a get-them-dead-or-alive justice. This only shows just how radical Jesus' call to love our enemies really is. To call this gently to the attention of a congregation in the midst of overwhelming popular support for retributive action requires uncommon courage, but it can also become an avenue to enable a deeper understanding of the gospel.[28]

Restorative justice moves beyond punitive justice; it requires making space for the other. There can be "no justice without the will to embrace" and "no genuine and lasting embrace without justice." This is because we believe that we belong to one another. If we reject this interrelatedness, each of us is left with his or her own justice, but not justice between us. This is not "about soft mercy tempering harsh justice, but about love shaping the very content of justice."[29] Restorative justice without love lacks both integrity and community.

> *Justice is rooted in interrelatedness; it is always about what is just in relations between people.*

One ethicist suggests that we need to start probing the meaning of justice in relation to various kinds of injustice. Injustice–and the responses to it–takes many different forms in different places, each with a different history. The response to the injustice of racial or sexist discrimination is quite different from the response to the injustice of institutionalized poverty. Justice in the latter case may call for redistribution (i.e., distributive justice) based on need or effort. What is due in terms of justice must be determined concretely, not in the abstract. This includes understanding the history behind the injustice: what contracts were coerced, how covenants were broken, and so forth. In addition, we will discover that injustice is a web of interlocking injustices. Race, gender, and poverty, for example, are not separate issues but are most often parts of a connected pattern.[30]

The often-pictured image of Justitia, a blindfolded angelic figure standing between a sword and a set of scales, is supposed to symbolize impartial justice, treating everyone equally and rising above special interests. This is hardly God's kind of justice, says Volf. God shows partiality to Israel (see Judg. 5:11 in light of 4:1); and within Israel God shows a particular concern for the widow, the orphan, the sojourner, and the poor (Ex. 22:21–27). "There is a profound injustice about the God of the biblical tradition. It is called grace." The prodigal son did not receive his due; he received the injustice of God's grace. God does not treat all people the same, but each person in his or her specificity.[31] No institutionalized justice that treats people purely within categories can deal with all the variable factors required by each situation seen in its historical development. If we want justice without injustice, we want love. From the perspective of God's reign, Justitia is able to see out of a heart of love. Then, loving one's enemy still results in justice.

> *"There is a profound injustice about the God of the biblical tradition. It is called grace."*

A theology of grace does not calculate differences and similarities between cases but seeks what is appropriate in each situation. Grace, of course, wants reconciliation. Receiving one's due means being reaccepted into the community, and this requires confession, moving beyond the threat of repeated violation, and being forgiven and reconciled. Punishing is not eliminated, but its imposition is toward reconciliation and embrace rather than for revenge. The justifying of the unjust is precisely what Paul proclaims in Romans 4:5. In light of our common humanity, loving and embracing the other define our approach to the complex particularities of exercising justice.[32]

THE PRINCIPLE OF JUSTICE APPLIED TO THE LATIMER CASE

Looking again at the Latimer case from a Christian sense of restorative justice, we seek to embrace Tracy, her parents–Robert and Laura–and their three other children. We look at all of them in their specificity and in their connectedness. Those concerned for the rights of disabled people need reassurance that the latter will be treated justly–that is, with fairness. It will not be achieved through a rigid application of regulations. As for Robert Latimer, the reconciliation that should be the goal of justice requires admission of wrong, confession, and a request for forgiveness. This does not substitute for punishment (including imprisonment), but it does call for more than self-defense. In the end, reconciliation recognizes that God is the giver of life and the One who enables us to transcend death. The will on Robert's part to embrace Tracy was both powerfully evident but also critically limited. He took her life. We as Christians must maintain the will to embrace Robert. Mary Anne Kasmeirski, a longtime advocate for integrated education for disabled people and mother of a son with Down's syndrome, affirmed him. What he did, she said, "he did out of compassion and out of love. I believe that, and I believe that a large number of Canadians believe that."[33] When we are open toward the other, we are better able to decide what justice requires.

> *"What does the LORD require of you / but to do justice, and to love kindness, / and to walk humbly with your God?" (Micah 6:8)*

Sermons on justice would do well to follow the example of Micah. When the prophet preached justice, he connected it with covenantal love and attentiveness to God (6:8). Three imperatives called Israel to see the world and the other as God sees them.[34] Preachers might offer back-to-back sermons: one on love of neighbor using a story like that of Tracy Latimer, followed by one on justice that wrestles with her father's action and resultant responses.

Ethics and Values and Assumptions

Keeping before us the larger question–How is our relationship before God reflected in what we are doing?–we move now to the way in which human behavior may be shaped by underlying values and basic assumptions about what is the good. How should we approach what we assume is the good? Dealing with a specific issue, how do we relate this to our assumptions about economics?

The relationship between moral values and behavior can be seen in a group of people who have responsibility together to make certain decisions. They find themselves unable to do so and are constantly bogged down in interminable, seemingly unresolvable arguments. Invited to reveal their personal values, they gradually discover what lies beneath their respective viewpoints. Eventually, they learn the difference between their own inclinations and preferences and those of the group. This enables them to explore shared values and move toward cooperation.

The scientific revolution of modernity distinguished between facts and values. Facts are admissible in the public arena, whereas values are regarded as personal and private.[35] Each person is entitled to his or her own values. Yet people also feel a need to share a core set of political values such as respecting others, protecting freedom of thought and religious belief, serving our communities, and refusing to steal or commit murder.[36]

So-called intrinsic values consist of primarily personal preferences such as happiness, pleasure, or good health. Extrinsic values are those goods that enable us to accomplish something else such as scientific research or the purchase of special hospital equipment. The common good has to do with broader shared public values: what is best for society as a whole.[37] Here, growing interest in corporate social responsibility emphasizes developing and revealing corporate values in the face of social and environmental pressures.[38]

From a Christian perspective, values are not just based on personal preferences, inherited social expectations, some decision-making consensus, or an agreement to resolve conflicts.[39] The good derives from the goodness of God. While creating the world, God repeatedly declared what the Creator had made to be good (Gen. 1). James reminds us that every good and perfect gift comes from God (Jas. 1:17). The church clarifies its understanding of personal and public good by reflecting on its faith.

> *Values are not just based on personal preferences, inherited social expectations, some decision-making consensus, or an agreement to resolve conflicts. The good derives from the goodness of God.*

Congregations need to have values concretized in two ways. One might be through a story of an individual like Chuck Collins. Born into a very wealthy Chicago family, he became co-director of a Boston-based advocacy group, United for a Fair Economy. The group's aim was to "cajole, pressure, and shame America's super rich" into giving away their tax windfalls to the country's forty million have-nots and to lobby against further tax breaks. Collins even went to the annual meeting of a large corporation to argue for a resolution to limit executive salaries, one in which the CEO received $83.6 million in salary and stock options the previous year. At this point the preacher might shift to a bit of commentary and say that Collins and the four hundred and fifty other members of his organization probably know that 10 percent of Americans have 73.2 percent of the wealth while the poorest 40 percent hold a mere one-half of 1 percent. Recently, we have also been informed that the average top CEOs in the U.S. now have compensation packages 310 percent higher than the average worker, up from 72 percent a decade ago. This is an issue of values.[40]

A second way a sermon could focus attention on values is to explore how corporations and many other organizations are developing statements of corporate values. The story of Tom's of Main could be told because its president, Tom Chappell, was so intent for his company to live by gospel values that he decided to enter Harvard Divinity School. He and the young MBAs who worked for him clashed over values. The young business experts focused on numbers, market share, and competition while Chappell cared more about the integrity of his products, service to customers, and other such matters. He wanted to discern how to utilize the skills of his executives and at the same time have them share deeper values. These would be in the interests of their company's highest values and would also be good business. With these kinds of details and a few more, the sermon might invite those interested in pursuing these matters further to undertake a serious study of Chappell's account of his company's journey.[41] Congregations want to live out Christian values, but they need examples–and also theological interpretation.

Ethics and Rights

Our final aspect of norms centers on claims that people believe they can justifiably make on others and on society, such as the right to live and be respected, to freedom and happiness, to assembly and free speech. Rights are sometimes also recognized for animals, not for their usefulness to human beings or the economy, but as sentient creatures, beings that have awareness and feelings.[42]

The recent so-called rights revolution is both fascinating and complex. Human rights charters such as the Constitution in the United States are protections against all forms of oppression, including those of the government and the legal system. But they are constantly being reinterpreted in light of particular circumstances. The kinds of rights emphasized in affluent countries have less to do with inequalities based on class and more to do with race, gender, and sexual orientation. By contrast, many developing nations are more focused on issues of equity and distribution of economic goods.[43]

Christian ethicists have argued from their doctrine of God's righteousness that all human beings and creation itself come under a universal law. They also see in the church a special type of social bonding based on law, hope, and love rather than family, ethnicity, or national power. God has gifted all persons with dignity, and this ought to be respected.[44] Lesslie Newbigin, in contrast, claims that the language of rights (as in the rights of freedom or equality) is inadequate. Political conservatives favor freedom and stress the satisfaction of wants. The political left focuses on equality and meeting basic needs, though these are often reduced to biological needs. So debates about the welfare state are interminable. In addition, respect, honor, and love cannot be claimed as rights. In the Bible's vision of human nature, relatedness is fundamental, rather than freedom or equality. When we take God's covenant seriously, respect, honor, and love are grounded in a profound mutuality. Congregations can recognize this relatedness for their own lives and also be invited to witness to it in the world.[45]

> *When we take God's covenant seriously, respect, honor, and love are grounded in a profound mutuality that grounds rights.*

Preaching on human rights can demonstrate this larger perspective of mutuality and the truth: We achieve rights by a power from beyond us, not from self-interest or even some well-founded collective interest. Congregations are quite willing to discover how our connections with one another and with the rest of God's creation can be evidenced. Preachers inspire insight and passion about these matters by retelling wonderful (and theological) vignettes drawn from novels such as Alan Paton's *Cry, the Beloved Country* or Joy Kogawa's *Obasan* and *Itsuka*.[46] Such stories can then be interpretively unpacked and connected to situations of human rights that are in the news. Nevertheless, congregations are simultaneously being influenced by the world's approach to human rights and may feel uncomfortable with sermons that raise such issues. For preachers faced with resistant listeners, William Sloane Coffin makes two suggestions. Make a careful study of those who are different from ourselves, and speak from the heart.[47]

In this chapter we have explored our obligations to God and one another by looking specifically at biblical norms, the principles of love and justice, underlying values and conceptions of the good, and finally, the rights and claims that are rooted in our understanding of human relatedness. Preaching ethics enables congregations to discern their obligations, to clarify their values, and to honor those rights that ought to be recognized in living out discipleship. But how will God's people do this in particular circumstances and specific contexts? To this question we now give our attention.

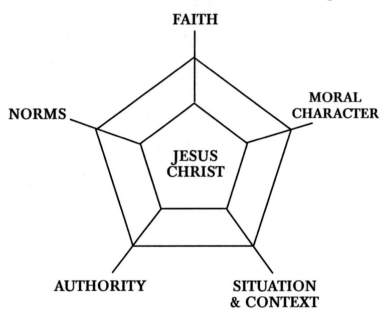

5

SITUATION AND CONTEXT
Preaching That Engages Particularity

Each Sunday as the congregation gathers for worship, they come both as people of faith and as persons and families situated in the midst of particular circumstances, decisions, and possibilities. These particularities are on their minds, influencing their participation and perhaps raising an expectation that their experience of worship will help make their lives more ethically (and spiritually) responsive. In previous chapters we have indicated that moral behavior is shaped by what we believe, is reflected in who we are, and is guided by the obligations of discipleship. But confronted by specific moral questions or decisions, how we ought to act may still not be obvious. Dietrich Bonhoeffer put the matter quite simply: Ethics is always "a matter of correct appreciation of real situations and of serious reflection upon them."[1]

Can our preaching contribute to ethical discernment? Can sermons enable listeners to look at their own circumstances or the larger context of their world through a gospel-based ethic? We believe we are called to live toward a new and alternative order. Our challenge is discerning the times, sorting through the facts, and then making concrete decisions.

In this chapter, therefore, we come to the section of our interconnected ethical web called situation and context. This is the fourth step in developing our approach to preaching ethics. We are seeking to answer the double question, What exactly is actually going on here, and how is our perception of it affected by the world around us? In doing so, we follow a three-stage process:

1. Gathering facts
2. Analyzing them in the larger context of our society
3. Assessing them from a Christian perspective

We will then apply this process both to a specific and personal decision in the area of medical ethics, and to the larger issue of poverty in society. Finally, we will turn our attention to how our attitudes toward gathering, analyzing, and assessing so-called facts are shaped by how we view the world. This will include asking how we may be influenced by cultural and ideological perspectives around us. Preaching frequently faces a barrier precisely at this point. Listeners may not hear what is being preached because the larger frame of reference is different for preacher and people, or because one or the other has been grasped more by the world's view of reality than by the gospel's. For example, preachers may find their most difficult challenge here if they believe that their moral conscience calls them to oppose war when their government and their media support it. Members of the congregation may believe that their moral conscience justifies war. On this and other very difficult questions, the sermon must seek to help both preacher and listeners wrestle with the biblical text—with the gospel—rather than with one another. This requires deep humility before God on the part of both preacher and congregation.

Ethics and Gathering Information

The first stage in facing ethical situations and their contexts is gathering basic information. Getting the facts is not as straightforward as it may seem, and preachers need to get their information straight. In chapters 1 and 2 the area of genetic studies opened up questions about the human genome project. A couple of years ago, scientists indicated that the human genome contains a hundred thousand genes. Several months later, that number was revised downward to between twenty-six and forty thousand. More recently still, the number seems to be thirty thousand. One wonders if the preacher has to check the Saturday paper in case some revision to Sunday's sermon needs to be made!

Preachers may prefer to stay with generalizations and statements of principle. That would be quite unfortunate. Congregations participate at a different level when preachers get into the particulars of a story. They feel narratives somewhere deep inside and begin to imagine how their faith can become moral action. Finding and using specific facts is a risk worth taking. The congregation will certainly permit and even applaud the risk-taking if the preacher does careful homework, admits limitations, and makes the distinction between fact and interpretation clear.

When sermons deal with concrete situations of importance to the church, listeners feel the narratives deep within and begin to imagine how faith can lead to moral action.

We—preacher and congregation—may not always be ready to face the "facts." In the late seventies someone gave me a copy of Ron Sider's *Rich Christians in an Age of Hunger*.[2] It took me several years before I dared to read it! I am not usually a procrastinator, but I intuitively felt it was going to make me feel guilty and discouraged— which it did! But I also ended up grateful for this work as a gift to help me listen to a biblical perspective on poverty.

One of my most liberating experiences in this regard came through a poignant image in Charles Elliott's *Praying the Kingdom*.[3] He describes a spring-loaded, sharp-toothed trap concealed under leaves waiting to seize its victim between the jaws of guilt and powerlessness. I could identify with those two feelings. Acknowledging them allowed an examination of each of them as spiritual forces and gave me a deeper awareness of countervailing spiritual resources in the discipline of prayer.

Sorting out the facts can still be a struggle, as it was for a couple in a fictional case presented on *Family Law*. How do we react when we see a television program about a difficult moral dilemma that could happen to us or to our neighbors? How might a sermon help the congregation to move to ethical reflection in such a situation?

Sorting Out the Facts: A Case in Medical Ethics

The show set the scene: A California couple recently had twin daughters joined together at birth and sharing vital organs.[4] The susceptibility of infection to one of them, and possible death for both, led to a moral confrontation. The hospital medical staff urged the couple to have the twins separated so that the stronger one could have a much better chance of surviving. When the couple refused to give their consent, the concerned hospital specialists went to court and asked a judge to rule that the best interests of the child most likely to survive should prevail over the wishes of the parents. The defense for the parents argued that it was possible that the two children might both be able to survive into their twenties, perhaps longer. The judge ruled that the parents themselves should decide.

The infants' medical state was stable, but one of them developed respiratory infections that flared up from time to time. The mother now believed the twins should be separated; the father disagreed. Back in court, specialists for each of the parents made their arguments, including a professional ethicist who stated that the separation of the twins was morally acceptable. The defense for the father objected to the presence of an ethicist, insisting that the judge was quite capable of knowing right from wrong. The judge allowed the testimony of the ethicist, but eventually he again refused to rule on the case. He said that he was not God. The parents had to decide.

The mother then applied for divorce and sued for custody of the children. A new court trial revealed new data, suggesting that other factors might lay behind the position each parent took. The mother had a career and didn't want the burden of caring for conjoined twins. The father felt that the death of their first child in a car accident was his fault and thus refused to take responsibility for another death. Whether or not any of this is fair, it raised the question of possible multiple motives on the part of the parents. This time the judge ruled in favor of the father. This devastated the father, as he now had full responsibility for the twins. When one child infected the other with a virus, the father finally agreed to the operation to save the stronger twin.

Sorting out the facts in this case requires expert witnesses, attempts to understand the motives of the parents, and weighing the interests of both of the infants against each other and alongside those of the parents. The struggle for discernment is not just scientific and personal; it is profoundly spiritual. This does not eliminate ambiguity, but it does pose an alternative to litigation. The giving up of life to save life is a biblical principle[5] that could have helped this couple face their dilemma rather than seek someone else to resolve it for them. Did the judge make the right decision in siding with the father? The television program implied that the father's subsequent change of mind allowed for a reconciliation that might have been far more difficult if the mother had been granted custody. But the mother's fight for the life of at least one of the infants appeared to be the better choice because the balance of good and bad consequences for the surviving infant was reflected in her position, as subsequent developments demonstrated. Did the story as told value the relationship between the parents over the welfare of one of the infants? Ambiguity forces the viewer to keep pondering the ethics of this case.

Sorting out the facts in difficult moral situations may not only be scientific and personal, it may also be profoundly spiritual.

THIS MIGHT BE RETOLD IN A SERMON AS FOLLOWS

God suffers when we suffer. In a heart-wrenching episode of the television program *Family Law*, a couple faced an excruciating decision. Their twin infant daughters were born joined together and sharing vital organs. One of them was susceptible to infections, making it likely that if they were not separated, both of them would die. An operation to separate them would certainly mean the death of the weaker twin. It was also possible that they both could survive for years if they remained fused together. What should the parents do?

In the television story, a series of court battles ensued between the hospital and the parents and between the parents themselves. Eventually, the battle dissolved the parents' relationship, and they separated. The judge did everything he could to put the decision in the hands of the parents, including finally choosing to award the children to the parent who stated a desire to forego an operation, to live on trust and against medical advice to let both twins live. In the end, however, the reality of the girls' precarious future led to a reversal of this decision. The twins were separated. One of them died; the other survived. The parents were reconciled. But this raises another ethical issue. Did the choice of the father as decision-maker reflect more concern for the couple than for the survival of one of their children?

None of us would want to be in the position of those parents, or of that judge, and perhaps not even of the lawyers involved in this case. But as Christians facing such decisions, we would be surrounded by another dimension: the upholding community of the church. We would also pray that through the expertise of professional persons acting with conscious ethical intent, we would be helped to discern God's way. We would be reminded by our faith in Christ that when we suffer, God suffers. In the midst of the sadness and mystery of death, the risen Christ affirms life, including life beyond death for the child whose life is taken so that her sister lives. In the end, our pain and suffering leads to a deeper faith, a stronger love. Would our faith and love, however, also make us willing to place the interests of a vulnerable infant ahead of ourselves?

Homiletically, we can now outline how the preacher engages in sermon formation.

1. The original story is reduced by more than a third. In this simplified form it is also more accessible.
2. The story is introduced theologically and so is already being transferred from a media piece into a sermon. Listeners start to anticipate the ethical dimension of the story in theological terms.
3. The reflection after the retelling[6] adds something that is entirely missing in a highly individualized culture–namely, the importance of a spiritual community for listeners who might find themselves facing a serious moral question.
4. We acknowledge the stewardship of experts–by implication, specialists in the congregation who are involved in these sorts of decisions are recognized for their moral role.
5. Finally, we sharpen the transcendent dimension. Life is seen through the cross and resurrection of Christ. We see God suffering with us when we suffer; we affirm life that transcends death. But the final question reminds us that faith can be tested by the most excruciating kinds of decisions.

Two cautions, however, need to be added. First, how does the preacher as pastor position this story knowing that some in the congregation may have had adverse pregnancy outcomes or children with disabilities? They might experience intense personal emotional reactions. Sermon stories frequently awaken other stories in the experience of the listeners. The preacher has to make a pastoral assessment about a given story's appropriateness and about how it will be introduced and told. Second, how will the story relate to a given text? One of the spiritual disciplines of ministers is the discernment of when a text is illuminated by such a story and when a story overshadows or moves in a direction different from the text. Congregations have a way of seeing such disconnects and can sense when storytelling reveals more about the storyteller than about the gospel.

Facts of Poverty–A Larger Societal Issue

At issue in this chapter is a double question, What exactly is actually going on in particular situations, and how is our perception of it affected by the world around us? We have focused primarily on a specific incident by looking at a domestic case. Now we want to probe a larger societal issue through an examination of statistics on poverty. In the United States, the 1996 signing of the Personal Responsibility and Reconciliation Act ended sixty years of open access to welfare. This welfare reform legislation limits welfare to five years in any one person's lifetime, even if part or all of that five years includes an individual's first five years of life. In a study of ten U.S. cities, 50 percent of families whose welfare benefits were reduced or eliminated became homeless.[7] This occurred in the decade of the 1990s when corporate profits rose by 116 percent and the pay increases of chief executive officers increased 535 percent (compared with 32 percent for ordinary workers).[8] In chapter 4 we noted that in 1999 the top 10 percent of the U.S. population had 73 percent of the wealth and that the bottom 40 percent had only one-half of 1 percent.[9] In Canada income disparities were also widening. At the turn of the century the richest 10 percent had 50 percent of the wealth while the bottom 40 percent had only 2.1 percent. Why do governments that have ample resources to ameliorate the condition of the poor enact legislation that appears to make them suffer more? Why do churches and other not-for-profit agencies often feel so helpless in the face of increasing levels of impoverishment? To respond to such questions, we turn to social analysis (stage 2), with the help of social science theory.

Ethics and Social Analysis

Postmodernist thinkers have pointed out that scientific claims (like so many others) are made from a given perspective. We as humans constantly analyze facts on the basis of human-constructed theories. Several such social theories have been used to determine what is wrong with society, and these influence responses to poverty.[10]

A functionalist sociology assumes that society is like a human body in which each organ has its own function. The basic problem with society is that the threat of social change or cultural disintegration can diminish personal freedom. Securing this equilibrium is more important than dealing with injustice. So a peaceful protest over government welfare policies is often met with riot police and turns into an uproar. The government then justifies its actions by appeals to equilibrium. The electorate chooses "peace" over demonstrations, even when these demonstrations may be in support of the defenseless.

A pluralist sociology sees many different conflicting centers of power in society and believes that we need political means for resolving the conflicts between them. Because one of the problems is the size of government bureaucracies, corporations, and labor unions, we should reduce the intrusion of bureaucracy in our lives, downsize governments, and limit labor unions. Welfare is viewed as being part of a bureaucratic structure, so reducing services seems desirable, even necessary. Of course, differences between various groups should be resolved through democratic processes. The poor would be more hopeful if these processes gave equal access to all income sectors, but governments increasingly treat citizens as taxpayers. They often listen more attentively in proportion to the amount of taxes paid (and frequently to those who make sizable political donations).

Dualist or conflict social theories place the problem of society in structures of oppression and domination. Economic differentials and controls are often central to conflict between the haves and have-nots. Other forms of oppression rooted in ethnic, racial, sexual, or religious discrimination are very real but often serve economic interests. Those in power (in government, business, or university) seek to persuade everyone that the view of the elite is the true understanding of society. What would benefit those on welfare are shifts both in economic power and in moral and intellectual leadership.

These broad theories offer differing explanations as to why affluent societies have many people living among them in poverty. Alongside these theories we need to probe a conflicting mix of assumptions about wealth and poverty:[11]

1. People have a right to well-being and to the means to exercise this right through adequate food, shelter, medical care, access to education, and the like. The state should make available productive employment opportunities and ensure that basic needs are met, even if this infringes (through graduated taxation) on the rights of others.
2. People are entitled to their wealth. They have a right to control, use, and dispose of this wealth as a fundamental freedom unless it has been derived through certain morally unacceptable means. As one journalist put it, "A proclivity to vote for parties that give away the money of other people in an attempt to help the poor is hardly creditworthy."[12]
3. The needs of the poor require that they have a certain social minimum standard of living. But this social minimum should not diminish commensurate incentives to ensure economic efficiency and appropriate savings.
4. People deserve what they get in society. Each is rewarded according to his or her contribution to society or to the economy. In its more extreme form, those in influential positions assume that they deserve greater rewards than others

do and, conversely, those who have the least are assumed to be undeserving even of what little they have.[13]

On closer examination of this fourth point, people do not get what they deserve. A person may be given a job or promotion based not on qualifications or performance but on the basis of friendship, seniority, or something else.[14] Even if people are rewarded on the basis of merit, rewards may not be commensurate with their contribution. In the last twenty years of the twentieth century, CEO salaries in the U.S. went from thirty-nine times the pay of the average worker to more than a thousand times,[15] which observers say does not come near reflecting their relative contributions. The notion of deserving does not take into consideration birth in one family and not another, educational advantages or disadvantages, good or bad health, or other factors beyond individual control. Even effort (often appealed to as a reason for differential rewards) is not free of certain advantages available only to some.

The preacher who engages in this kind of analysis will immediately recognize the need for careful language. Listeners may hold one or another of these perspectives without having reflected critically on them. Many will appreciate the opportunity to do so if it is presented in a thoughtful and non-accusatory way. Here, the issue is not whether people are indifferent to poverty, but that they have distinct views of what causes it. The sermon is not about attacking the motives of people but helping them reflect on how they analyze such a problem, including their implicit theory of society. The point of the sermon is to help the congregation come to insight as to whether this or that way of analyzing the facts is adequate in dealing with the reality of poverty rather than affirming (or challenging) the preconceived views of listeners.

The sermon is not about attacking the motives of people, but helping them reflect on how they analyze such a problem, including their implicit theory of society.

Ethics and Assessment of Analysis

Having looked at fact-gathering and social analysis, we turn now to formulating an assessment (stage 3), using the issue of poverty once again. As churches look at the existence of poverty, their biblical heritage (in which this is a pervasive and central trajectory) obligates them to engage it. Exodus tells how a group of Hebrew peoples were liberated out of a situation of slavery in Egypt. Early in its life, Israel articulated laws that emphasize God's demand that the poor and the vulnerable be cared for.[16] True religion, according to Isaiah 58, centers on sharing bread with the hungry and welcoming the homeless. After the exile in the fifth century B.C.E., Governor Nehemiah confronted the nobles over their exploitation of the poor. They reformed their economic arrangements, restored lands, and ceased to charge interest from their poorer Jewish neighbors (Neh. 5). When the disciples of John the Baptist asked for signs of messiahship, Jesus included "good news for the poor" (Mt. 11:5, author's trans.). In the parable of the last judgment (Mt. 25), people are admitted into the kingdom or are rejected depending on whether they have cared for "the least of these."[17] So how does the church respond to poverty?

Recently, the U.S. government invited churches to be involved in "faith-based" programs to address poverty. Carl Dudley sees in this an opportunity to demonstrate that "welfare reform is a faith issue" and not just an economic one. He takes us back several centuries to the European transition from an agrarian barter system to an urban market economy. At that time the Protestant Reformers regarded unemployment as an offence to God. Everyone in society has gifts from God, and these are to be used in productive employment. The issue for us today is moving from dependency on welfare to responsible participation in society.[18] This transition is not just psychological and educational; it is also spiritual. The chronically poor, who have often grown up in poverty and have little or no other experience, may tend to live just for today. The gospel has the power to enlarge their vision, especially through the community support of the church. This journey requires conversion to hope not only on the part of those who are poor but also for the volunteers who work with them. Each person's value is rooted in grace, and grace transcends all distinctions between who is worthy and who is not in society.[19]

This is the personal dimension. It echoes, in a way, Lesslie Newbigin's concern to focus not on rights versus needs but on our relatedness in Christ. Gordon Graham has argued in a similar way against appeals for justice, which he contrasts with *charitas* (grace). He shows that today's use of "justice" arises out of seventeenth- and eighteenth-century social contract theories. It is primarily public, with a focus on rights, and is notoriously hard to implement legally. This concern with poverty as a right is stressed to defend personal dignity. Because dignity is connected with self-reliance, this fits well with liberal individualism. If, however, we start with the equal worth of all people, responding to the needs of others does not diminish their dignity.

Our dignity resides neither in ourselves nor in our autonomy, but in God in whose image we are created. This gives rise to *charitas*, a benevolence that does not rely on justice as understood by our culture. Such benevolence rests solely on the love of Christ, who calls us to love our neighbor as ourselves.[20]

Accepting this distinction does not mean that the church should not work alongside other social groups in the struggle for a fairer and more just economic order.[21] For example, the church could express support for a Toronto lawyer who proposed a way of increasing access to the legal system for people of modest incomes who cannot afford high-priced lawyers. He asked judges to award legal costs on the basis of the relative difference in incomes between litigants. This, the lawyer contended, would likely reduce the influence of the marketplace on the legal system and increase accessibility to justice for ordinary citizens.[22]

The spiritual dimension of poverty, however, is part of a much larger issue: the reign of death by principalities and powers. William Stringfellow argues that this reign of death is not only manifested in the literal sense of the slaughter of innocent victims in war, but it also takes on a social form "in the banishment or abandonment of human beings to loneliness, isolation, ostracism, impoverishment, unemployability, separation..." These victims of the powers become so dehumanized that they "suffer few illusions about their consignment to death, or to these moral equivalents of death by American society."[23] Ultimately, preaching does not assume that poverty is eradicated even by the best of human, or even the church's, efforts. It requires God's redeeming activity, and this, in turn, calls for earnest prayer and resistance to the powers as spiritual forces.

> *Ultimately, preaching does not assume that poverty is eradicated even by the best of human, or even the church's, efforts. It requires God's redeeming activity.*

Situation and Context–The Preaching Task

Gathering, analyzing, and assessing data for moral decisions is often extraordinarily challenging. A sermon of fifteen, or even twenty-five, minutes is not adequate to the task of looking carefully at a theme such as poverty or welfare reform. But preaching is not an isolated event; it is a journey over months and years. This allows us to weave aspects of such a theme in and out of our sermons, so that the larger picture emerges over time.

Four suggestions might assist the preacher in the weaving process:

1. A fairly extensive study of poverty could be the focus of one year; health care or genetic research could receive attention in subsequent years. Developing a file for newspaper clippings (indexed in a computer file) could indicate what keeps on being raised in the consciousness of the congregation.
2. The preacher may engage the congregation in the process of discovery. Some members have expertise that could provide special information. Others may cut out news items (because we do not all read the same papers or magazines) and participate in a study group on a chosen theme.
3. The sharper the contrast between contemporary culture and the gospel, the more the preacher will want to invite the congregation to give candid feedback. The sermon is not a consumer product designed to meet consumer demand, but a proclamation that graciously trusts the work of the Spirit among the people of God. Such preaching can be a struggle, but the struggle is not between preacher and congregation. The struggle is between preacher and congregation on one hand and the call of the gospel on the other.
4. Sermons should move beyond explanation and analysis to the actual lives of people. Congregations are awakened through their imaginations. Stories and images can penetrate and transform us as we hear the cries that God hears.

Ethics and Worldview

In our examination of this fourth area of preaching ethics, which we have called "situation and context," we have kept in mind the double question, What is actually going on here, and how is our perception of it affected by the world around us? Part of that "world around us" is its mindset or worldview. This is critically important to help preachers grapple with the puzzling reality that sometimes, in spite of their best efforts, their listeners just don't seem to "get it."

Why is it that sometimes congregations listen to gospel proclamation and just don't seem to "get it"?

In the film *Patch Adams* (based on a true story), a medical student confronts the worldview of his medical school professors, who state that specialists are needed to treat people in their feeling of dependency. Their condition must be objectified. This will avoid subjective involvement on the part of the doctor, who can then treat the illness scientifically. Patch Adams views the medical profession differently. He sees it as a way of helping people in their time of need, enabling them to be involved in their own healing. Everyone is both patient and doctor. Every doctor, accordingly, has to become personally involved in order to heal. Points of tension between these two worldviews of medical practice are evident. Are human beings fundamentally good or profoundly flawed? Is death the enemy (hence, its arrival constitutes medical failure) or part of life (in which case the doctor then seeks to help the dying face it)?

The sharpest clarification of ideological differences is presented toward the end of the movie. A dramatic "sermon" is preached before a medical court but addressed primarily to the larger assembled "congregation." What is particularly significant about this sermon is that it follows the living out of Patch Adams' alternative perspective in the lives of human beings. We hear his point of view in relation to lived experience and make our judgment about its validity accordingly.

In looking at the facts of life around us in this chapter, we have already admitted that our sight-lines are limited by our finitude, our socialization, and our acculturation—the latter two are shaped by our view of the world. We ask the faith question about how to see what we are called to see, and in response, we need to clarify what we mean by "ideology." This term is sometimes used positively as a perspective on the world that increases our vision and hopefulness, but more often negatively as a distortion and limitation that prevents us from seeing truly.[24]

Coming to a Larger Consciousness

Sometimes we have experiences that expand our consciousness. When students of the Bible in the late 1970s read works such as Phyllis Trible's *God and the Rhetoric of Sexuality*,[25] they became aware in a new way of the role of gender in interpretation. Once awakened, we begin a whole new process of discovery. Rebecca Chopp calls this rereading of Christian theology from a feminist perspective "saving work." As a process of reconstructing patterns of communication from patriarchal enslavement to freedom in community, this shift reflects "the goal, activity and being of God in the world."[26] Language evolves out of social relationships that can reflect either control or openness. A new awareness, what Paulo Freire calls *concientizacion*, requires not only a recognition that the world is seen differently, but also a willingness to express it differently.[27] The language we use in preaching is never neutral; it is either a channel of saving work or a wall against it, not only with reference to gender but also for other relationships. The use of language is an ethical issue.[28]

This positive sense of the term "ideology" is a symbolic act of imagination rooted in a desire to be as open to God and God's world as one can. It is not just an individual projection but the corporate hope of a believing community to accept correction as well as the unexpected. Such a worldview can incorporate new insights, for example, from the field of quantum science. Walter Wink, in his expansive treatment of the powers, begins with a series of diagrams on the relationship between heaven and earth. The differences in these worldviews advance our ability to understand how the powers are seen to operate and how God and the world are connected or disconnected. As a result, we can discern the ethical reality of power grounded in faith.[29]

Ideology as False Consciousness

Ideology used in a negative sense is the opposite of this expanding openness to God's world. Jon Sobrino writes about moving to El Salvador in 1957 and witnessing appalling poverty. He says, "Even though I saw it with my eyes, I did not really see it. Thus that poverty had nothing to say to me." He could have said that he was locked into a false consciousness—which left him impervious to the realities of poverty all around him. Candidly, he admits that all his years of study "hadn't taken from me the heart of stone I had for the suffering of this world." But in 1974 he began "to awaken from the sleep of inhumanity." Through a community of people he was able to see that "truth, love, faith, the gospel of Jesus, the very best that we have as people of faith and as human beings—these are somehow to be found among the poor."[30]

Some Christians would speak of their transformation from a secularist to a Christian perspective as conversion.[31] This would be consistent with Romans 12:2 and other passages that speak about turning from the way the world perceives reality to seeing through the influence of God's Spirit (1 Cor. 2:6–8). To assume, however, that a commitment to follow Jesus Christ automatically breaks the power of cultural ideologies that distort reality is naïve.[32]

False consciousness masks what is really going on in the world. It prefers its own theoretical constructs and evokes the power of symbols and structures often associated with political or economic power. Ideology in this sense is not just the subjective preferences of people with whom one disagrees. Ideology is an expression of the influence of fallen principalities in shaping how a given community faces the world and is committed to this perspective no matter what others say.[33] One can understand the outrage that followed the terrorist attacks of 9/11 and appreciate the expressions of profound sorrow the President, the mayor of New York City, and the nation expressed to bring healing and hope. But the "war on terrorism" gradually morphed into a larger militarization project with extraordinary security measures in the U.S. and eventually a unilateral declaration of war against Iraq, a country that, as it turns out, was not the threat to the U.S. as claimed. Some have pointed out that this development was so ideological that voices of dissent often seemed almost impossible to hear.[34] Nor was it possible to explore the larger picture of terrorism elsewhere in the world, such as in Columbia, Guatemala, Zimbabwe, and Sudan. History, accordingly, was diminished rather than being used as a lens through which to review this terrible tragedy. Ideology, it would seem, had gained the upper hand.[35]

Preaching in the wake of 9/11 was an awesome challenge. Reflecting on four books of sermons that shared this struggle, Methodist pastor Mark Horst states that the sermons that "worked best here are the ones that are rough and incomplete: that have jagged edges, that fail to comfort; that fail to bring closure."[36] Congregations need honesty, an opportunity to stand raging with the psalmists, weeping with Jesus, longing for a new creation with Paul (Rom. 8), and, yes, praising with the community of faith. Walter Brueggemann's words about preaching come to mind: "not instruction, rational discourse, or moral suasion" but "the invitation and permit to practice a life of doxology and obedience." Doxology is what enables the congregation to "dare a move out of fearful muteness."[37]

> *The post-9/11 sermons that work best "are the ones that are rough and incomplete: that have jagged edges, that fail to comfort; that fail to bring closure."*

Elsewhere, Brueggemann clarifies in more detail why doxology is so central in the church's life in relation to ideology. He sees a link between ideology and idolatry. An ideological perspective is one that "will not change and cannot be criticized." It seeks the support of "civil religion in which the living God becomes the patron of the status quo," so that the present system feels very much like the kingdom of God. In this idolatrous stance we deny God's transcendent power and act as though it's all up to us and our powers. Over against ideology and idolatry, Brueggemann invites the church to engage in re-symbolization, in an act of "world-making as an imaginative enterprise."[38] So in an Epiphany homily he offers a vivid contrast between the great pretensions of Jerusalem and the modest promises of Bethlehem, between a text that evokes security and prosperity (Isa. 60) and one about vulnerability and peace (Mic. 2).[39] Colleague Chuck Campbell stresses that Brueggemann's sermons are "passionate about God"; he "unapologetically proclaims the 'odd' God of the Bible," one who is intrusive, particular, and active in the world.[40] Doxology enables congregations to see through ideology because doxology is the ultimate stance of openness to the God of truth.

It may be especially helpful at this time to reflect on Martin Luther King Jr.'s sermon, "Beyond Vietnam," preached in Riverside Church, New York, exactly one year before his assassination. King began by acknowledging that he was opposing U.S. government policy and confronting America's "apathy of conformist thought."[41] He noted that the issues in this case were so perplexing that one is mesmerized by uncertainty. The call to speak is "a vocation of agony." But he was emboldened by the fact that many religious leaders have moved beyond "patriotism to the high grounds of a firm dissent based upon the mandates of conscience and the reading of history"–a history of American unwillingness to support Vietnam's independence after World War II. In these words King self-consciously confronted ideology. He knew its power and cunning; he also saw its weakness. The ideology of this war contradicted both moral conscience and human history.

Regarding the Vietnam War, Martin Luther King Jr. said that he was emboldened by the fact that many religious leaders had moved beyond patriotism to the high ground of dissent based on mandates of conscience.

Next, King turned to make the connection between his fight for racial dignity in the U.S. and the Vietnam War. He stated that the War on Poverty program, launched with such promise by President Lyndon Johnson, had been totally undermined by the military industrial complex (vividly described later in the sermon). His own people would pay a high price, including the deaths of a sharply disproportionate number of black Americans in Vietnam. But at a deeper level the war flew in the face of King's own commitment to nonviolent ways of resolving conflict.

At the heart of his sermon King appealed to the gospel as a message of grace for all people, without distinction. Integral to this larger vision was King's urgent plea to see this conflict from the perspective of the brutality and madness of war. This included both the terrible suffering of the Vietnamese people and also the deaths of American troops. King quoted former President Kennedy, "Those who make peaceful revolution impossible will make violent revolution inevitable." Scripture repeatedly calls us to love one another (Jn. 13:34; 15:12, 17; Rom. 12:10; 13:8; 1 Thess. 4:9; 1 Pet. 1:22; 1 Jn. 3:11, 14, 23; 4:7, 11–12; 2 Jn. 1:5). That is the alternative vision to the ideology of war and the motivation to struggle for a new world.[42]

What Martin Luther King Jr. preached in this sermon was contrary to his political instincts and in the face of overwhelming opposition both within the civil rights movement and outside of it.[43] One cannot help but realize that the power of ideology as impervious to change or criticism can be massively overpowering[44] —except to the persistent liveliness of the gospel. Proclaiming such a word of grace has nothing to do with trying to meet the (consumer) expectations of listeners, and everything to do with faithfulness to a calling from beyond ourselves. The source of hope is not in the Martin Luther Kings of the pulpit (though we deeply admire his courage), but in the Spirit who awakens in us God's alternative order and enables us to share it. Nora Tubbs Tisdale, in a candid reflection, says, "The Gospel we don't want to hear (or preach)" helps us see the preacher's struggle when a text does not resonate with one's personal inclinations.[45]

Homiletics, as we have noted repeatedly in this chapter, is "an event in transformed imagination." In this particular aspect of ethical preaching it is all too easy to become strident and accusatory. What is called for here is poetry that voices the world differently and invites the congregation to a new conversation. "The deep places in our lives—places of resistance and embrace—are not ultimately reached by instruction." They require stories and metaphors, imaginative alternatives of how we Christians view the world through the tear-filled eyes of Jesus on a scandalous cross. It is this that will evoke a new conversation that has room "for ambiguity, probe and daring hunch."[46]

We set out in this chapter to probe the particular circumstances and societal contexts in which we make ethical decisions. The double question before us has been, What exactly is actually going on here, and how is our perception of it affected by the world around us? We developed a way for preachers to gather information, analyze it, and assess it. In the process we became conscious of the ways our perspectives are shaped by how we view the world, and saw preaching as an invitation to a new (gospel) way of seeing. By what authority do we do this? To what do we appeal? These now require our attention.

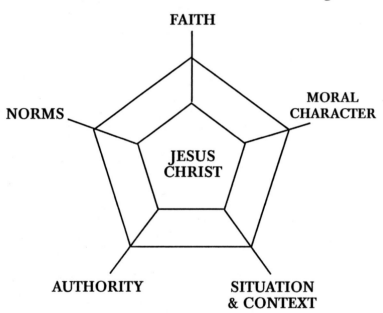

6

AUTHORITY

To What Do Preachers Appeal?

From a Christian perspective the music of ethics is about God's purpose and will. But where is this purpose and will disclosed most reliably? What avenues of revelation give substance to moral reflection?[1] As we have moved through the various areas of our interconnected ethical web, we have been anticipating this chapter. Passages of scripture, stories of the experiences of people, references to scientific studies, references to traditions that shape our thinking, and ways of reasoning have all been woven through our discussions. The substance of what has been written rests on some source of authority like various parts of an orchestra appealing to a musical score.

In this chapter we invite preachers to wrestle with the question, To what are we appealing when we express our viewpoints? In this the fifth step in developing our approach to preaching ethics, we look specifically at four classical authorities:

1. experience
2. reason
3. tradition
4. scripture

hold this as an important work for you always

Beyond their use as sources of authority, we ask how they are interactive, though weighted differently.² In our exploration of the authority of scripture we include a fourfold process of interpretation to show how ancient biblical texts may ground the proclamation of the gospel. Delving into the four authorizations, we illustrate how each functions in relation to such conflictive debates as those on abortion, homosexuality, and domestic violence. This is not intended to solve such debates but to clarify how the appeal to one authority or another affects the reflective process.

Preachers might bring to this exploration a series of questions:

- **What authority do you tend to appeal to in your preaching?** What forms of authorization do you avoid or see as of lesser value? How might this be related to your socialization and your theology?
- **What authority do your listeners expect?** How does this fit or clash with your own? What do you do when such clashes occur?³
- **How is the question of authority different today than it was fifty years** ago and why?⁴

With such issues in our consciousness, we turn to our various sources of authority.

Ethics and the Authority of Experience

Preachers seek to portray experience in terms of God's presence and out of their awareness of the world. Experience can be viewed personally–what persons and groups encounter in life–and also through the lens of empirical studies. Both are used in church debates about homosexuality. For some, experience needs to be correlated with other forms of authorization; for others, experience is the primary channel for discovering one's moral path. Our beginning point for exploring these issues is theology, particularly our doctrines of human nature, God's providence and sanctifying grace, and God's Spirit.

God's Gift of Experience and the Example of Grace

The psalmist experienced doxology while gazing at the night sky. Without speech or words, a sense of God's presence enveloped his whole being (Ps. 19:1–3). When the disciples of John the Baptist asked Jesus on behalf of John if he were the Messiah, Jesus pointed to experience: "Tell John what you hear and see" (Mt. 11:4). The apostle John echoed this when he wrote about apostolic preaching, "We declare...what we have heard, what we have seen with our eyes, what we have looked at and touched with our hands, concerning the word of life" (1 Jn. 1:1).[5]

Because we are, by our very nature, connected with God, we should not be surprised that our experiences can be a source of discerning God's way. Sometimes a preacher turns to experience to illuminate the ethical import of the gospel, as in Fred Craddock's sermon, "My Mother's Name Is Grace."[6] He tells of worshiping in a village church one Sunday, a church about which he knew nothing. It was filled, and he sensed an air of expectation. As the choir moved forward, he caught his first glimpse of the preacher. "I was not prepared for what I saw," he admits. As the preacher ascended the pulpit, Craddock noted, "one eye was not in concert with the other, and both of them had a milky film over them; and he had very thick lenses for his glasses. When he spoke, the muscles in his neck were visible and strained as though speaking is something that he learned as an adult, not as a child." But something happened as he preached. There was a deep pastoral dimension, a caring that was both firm and tender. How, Craddock wonders, did it happen that this person was so obviously loved, respected, and listened to?[7]

> *Sometimes a preacher turns to experience to illuminate the ethical import of the gospel.*

At the end of the service as the preacher was shaking hands, one woman said, "I wish I knew your mother." To which the preacher responded, "My mother's name is grace." Craddock later asked the pastor about this reference to his mother. The preacher told him that his mother gave him up at birth. He was in an institution and then moved from foster home to foster home. He could have been adopted, "but as you can tell, nobody would adopt me. But when I was a teenager, I went with a group of young people to a church, and there I met grace."

Craddock then explains in his own sermon that this was not just saving grace, beautiful as that is. This was *sanctifying grace,* "the grace of God working in the mind and heart of a person quietly, gradually over the years until it makes you a gracious person," affecting your values and all your relationships. As a result you act with generosity, struggle for justice, and in many other ways evidence that "your mother's name is grace."

This sermon appeals to experience. Through his own, Craddock discerned in another a gospel of grace that evidences moral virtue, points to acts of quiet generosity, and reveals a community of uncommon mutual acceptance. In the process Craddock's uncomfortable description of the pastor makes us as listeners deal with our own moral prejudice toward people with disabilities. Redemption comes only at the sermon's end through the vignette about the conversations at the door after the service. References to experience stand out in this sermon, but it also appeals to scripture and the church's tradition of sanctifying grace. Thus, scriptural authority and the authority of church tradition contribute significantly to the sermon's interpretation of experience.

Discerning the Holy Spirit

Discerning God in experience is not easy. Indeed, for this we need a *doctrine of the Holy Spirit*. Michael Welker argues that the Spirit is not some form of common sense, moral sensibility, or feeling of right and wrong. The Spirit mediates God's presence and will. This means that "no human experience is in control of God *as such*." We need "new ways to examine past, present and future experiences and expectations of God, testing them for their connections and differences." Our discernment will be assisted by "concentrating on the 'primary testimonies' of the biblical traditions and the secondary testimonies in our cultures."[8] For these reasons we are encouraged "[not to] believe every spirit, but test the spirits to see if they are from God" (1 Jn. 4:1). Appeals to the authority of the Spirit, therefore, are best viewed within one's experience of God and need to be made with due caution and humility.

> *The Spirit is not some form of common sense, moral sensibility, or feeling of right and wrong. Discerning how the Spirit works in our experience requires caution, humility, and community.*

Discerning the Spirit requires community. Rebecca Chopp speaks of an "*ekklesia* of grace." Like other Christian feminists, she believes in "spaces of grace for experiencing and creating new forms of relationship with God, self, others, and the world."[9] This includes a spirituality of connectedness. Recently, a woman in our congregation was diagnosed with cancer. She gave our pastor permission to share with the congregation the struggle she faced in the coming week, including the possibility of a difficult operation. When our pastor came down and helped us pray with her and her family, I (and, I believe, many others) experienced the *ekklesia* of grace.

Authority 103

Preachers can draw on their own intuitions and pay attention to their own emotions to guide them in these delicate matters.[10] This does not obviate the need for assessing the appropriateness of drawing on experience because preachers are seeking to discern the *Spirit's* impulse. They also take seriously and respond accordingly to their listeners as those who embody a community of experiences.

Appealing to Empirical Studies of Experience

When we try to understand human life and how God may be involved in our lives, we may also appeal to empirical studies in newspaper stories, books, and journal articles. Such studies fall between experience and reason because they draw directly on human experience and are also a form of reasoning about the data gathered. In the area of human sexuality these have broadened our awareness and indicated how it may be understood quite differently today from biblical times. Lisa Sowle Cahill looks at such studies and asks, "What does the increasingly plentiful data about the frequency and etiology of a human phenomenon like homosexuality 'prove' about its moral character?" Empirical studies can tell us a lot about many aspects of sexuality, she responds, but based on description they cannot "tell us conclusively what place such factors *ought* to have...The decisive question for Christian ethics is which 'naturally' occurring and even functionally 'healthy' facts, states, and relations also represent moral ideals." For this, she concludes, we need to turn to scripture, tradition, and normative accounts of the human.[11]

Empirical studies may be referred to in a sermon, though cautiously, because our surrounding culture often uses quantitative data without adequate critical reflection.

Preachers may wonder about how much time they can invest in this kind of research. There may be various ways to work collaboratively with members of the congregation or other pastors when a particular issue seems especially important to the life of the church. Empirical studies may be referred to in a sermon, though cautiously, because our surrounding culture uses quantitative data without the kind of critical reflection demonstrated by Cahill. James Gustafson has sharpened our awareness of the problems associated with empirical studies by asking what data is relevant to specific moral issues, their principles of interpretation, and their normative biases.[12] We might well wonder if such factors make deliberation of this kind more appropriate in a church study series rather than in a sermon. Yet the larger societal perspectives on moral questions are often in the minds of the listening congregation. Making some reference to them in sermons can be helpful, especially when these are evaluated through appeals to other authorities.

Ethics and the Authoritative Appeal to Reason

We continue to explore the question, To what are we appealing when we express our viewpoints? We have looked at experience; now we turn to reason. The first great commandment includes loving God with all our *minds* (Mk. 12:30). The gift of the Spirit enables Christians to have "the *mind* of Christ" (1 Cor. 2:16, author's emphasis). When Paul turned to the ethical portion of his letter to the Romans, he urged a renewing of their *minds* (Rom. 12:2). Preachers need to be able to make well-reasoned ethical arguments if they want congregations to grapple with what they say. Some ethicists view reason as "a source of God's revelation itself"; to others, reason is "a way of making sense of divine teachings."[13] We look at each of these and seek to illustrate them homiletically.

Preaching That Appeals to Reason as a Source of Insight

Theologically, it is possible to use reason as a source in ethics because of common grace. We are made with a capacity to know God and to understand right from wrong. The mystery here requires humility, notes Max Stackhouse. Such humility allows one's vision of truth to be tested by reason itself. "Grace may be the keystone," but it "holds little together if it is disconnected from the arch stones of reason, morality, and society."[14] Human sinfulness can distort but not destroy this capacity.[15] In discussing the moral nature of the universe, Nancy Murphy and George Ellis conclude that our response to God's world and to God must reflect God's nature as essentially *self-emptying*. This implies "an awareness of our status relative to God that enables an emptying of our pride in relation to our work" and to people that we encounter. "This awareness is what ultimately makes a kenotic ethic achievable." Reason cannot be used even to imply some superiority on our part toward God. Reason in Christian ethics flows out of a humble walk with God.[16]

> *Reason in Christian ethics flows out of a humble walk with God.*

In seeking to be open to reason as a source of insight, the preacher may get a new angle of vision. We can illustrate this in relation to the controversial subject of abortion and recent genetic studies. Archbishop John Habgood, who is also a trained physiologist, explains the crucial point at which a fetus "can be said to have a firm identity" (around fourteen days after conception). This means two things. Before that point the union of sperm and egg is "no more than a chemical reaction, albeit a wonderfully mysterious and potent one." After this period the cells differentiate themselves into the person-to-be. Distinctive personhood begins to develop in responsiveness to the mother's womb. As this happens, an awareness of an *other* like ourselves grows. With it comes moral responsibility toward that *other*. This responsibility may be in tension with the desire on the part of some parents to be tested for the possibility of genetic defects, namely after the fourteen-day period. At what point would a therapeutic abortion appear justified and be "a moral option, too, despite objections against interfering with genetic givenness?"[17]

A sermon usually addresses a congregation that includes people with different viewpoints on therapeutic abortion.[18] Such a sermon might begin something like this:

> As a community of God's people, I assume that all of us finally find our fulfillment in response to God. But what does this mean for a couple faced with a difficult decision regarding therapeutic abortion? Suppose this couple has discovered through genetic testing that their expectant child has a high chance of having a most debilitating disease. All of this is very personal, but we as Christians are also part of a body of people who seek mutual support and discernment together. So how can we ponder the implications of recent genetic developments and assess their impact on our thinking?

[At this point the sermon could summarize (and simplify) Archbishop Habgood's analysis. The sermon might then continue by drawing the congregation's attention to the new questions that this raises for them.]

> What should we do with the tension posed by Archbishop Habgood's question? Does science now open up new options for couples, and how are they to choose which ones to follow? These are challenging questions, and we should be grateful for the new knowledge that genetic studies offer us. We should

also ponder these issues together for one another and for the world that does not always pursue the more ultimate implications of scientific research for grasping our true humanness before God. It would be good to convene a study on therapeutic abortion because this sketch is all too brief. But for now, I would like us to reflect further on our Christian understanding of human nature to clarify how we might face difficult decisions like the one I have just described.

[The preacher might then use "natural reason" to show what is consistent with our nature as God's creatures. Such reasoning as a source of moral authority should, of course, include theological reflection.]

Reason as a Way of Discerning the Implications of Scripture

Another way of appealing to reason is to view it as a way of discerning the implications of scripture. On this view "unaided" reason requires special revelation because of human sinfulness. Here, a preacher might ask, "Are you among those who reject science as a source of primary authority in these matters but are prepared to agonize with parents who are fearful of the consequence of not aborting a fetus that could eventually be a suffering child?" The sermon could then ground thinking about human nature in Genesis 1 and 2. You should pay special attention to Exodus 21:22–23, which seems to distinguish between abortion and murder. You should also deal with the sanctity of life implied in the birth stories of Jesus.[19] These passages still leave considerable room for reasoning because they do not deal specifically with new information arising from genetic research. But it is now clear that the authority of reason is diminished because it is subservient to another authority.

> *Reason in Christian ethics needs to be subservient to the authority of scripture and the ongoing life of the church.*

Those who seek to reason *within* the authority of scripture may see this as part of the self-emptying or as implied in the walking humbly with God noted above. They may also see that these dispositions take place within the life of the church and its ongoing journey of interpretation. Such dispositions toward scripture are integrally linked to the formation of the canon of scripture and the experience of the ancient biblical communities that shared their faith. Entering into the reasoning of this distant biblical world could require a radical shift in perspective.[20] In light of these different approaches to reason, preachers will want to clarify for themselves and their listeners just how reason is appealed to as an authority.

Ethics and the Authority of Tradition

Sometimes reason aligns itself with or gives way to tradition. Preachers live within traditions and inevitably both draw on them and appeal to them. The congregation is a traditioned community; it lives in some way out of its history. Tradition cannot be taken for granted; indeed, it already begins in the Bible.

Tradition in the Bible and the Church

The formation of the library of biblical books over many centuries reveals the flexibility of tradition in Ancient Israel and the early church. The covenant tradition is a case in point. The Mosaic covenant, reaching back to Sinai, established a relationship between the LORD and the Hebrew people; it was a conditional summons to obedience (Ex. 19). Israel was to both obey and find direction through Torah, God's law. Several centuries later Torah was reinterpreted for new circumstances. When the monarchy appeared to introduce a royal covenant without qualification (2 Sam. 7; Ps. 89), this was modified in the tradition with the "if you obey" of Torah (1 Kings 3:14; 9:4–8; Ps. 132). Still later during the exile, Torah was given a new future orientation enabling God's people to keep Torah as a new covenant (Jer. 31:33; Ezek. 36:26–27).[21] Hebrews 8 gave this covenant tradition a final application, identifying Jesus Christ as the mediator of the new covenant. This dynamic, creative movement of tradition cautions us against thinking of tradition as fixed and unimaginative!

> *The dynamic, creative movement of tradition cautions us against thinking of tradition as fixed and unimaginative!*

Wogaman's reflections on the history of the church's ethical positions should not surprise us: "Christians have arrived at opposite conclusions about many things, such as war, slavery, the role of women, wealth, sexual relationships, politics, and even the more commonplace virtues." Could it be otherwise, as tradition witnesses to the living God? But within all of this diversity and necessary development, "tradition has always affirmed the centrality of love in the nature of God and in the character of human life."[22] Love, to be sure, has not always been evident in the church's decisions and behavior, but the ideal remains. From this central conviction, as well as in its struggle for discernment on many other matters, the church continues to include reflection on tradition in its moral discourse. Sometimes that tradition will challenge present tendencies; sometimes new insights will critique tradition. Wogaman, therefore, notes, "Too much certainty about God's ways with humanity may not leave enough room for God to be God."[23]

Preaching Depends on Tradition amid Traditions

We have seen that intractable moral disputes have consistently marked ethical debate. Such disputes should be evidence enough that modernity was living a myth when it posited universal norms of behavior. This is not just a matter of the inadequacy of our debates, says Alasdair MacIntyre. Rather, it arises because we all live out of specific traditions that we have inherited. We do not make decisions merely as individuals. Our decisions are embedded in larger social traditions, each of which has a sense of the good and a way of sustaining internal conflicts. Such traditions are strengthened through the exercise of moral virtues. Discerning right from wrong arises not from abstract thought or some intuitive choice, but from understanding the story of our lives within a larger tradition.[24] To find our identity in a moral community that traditionalizes us does not mean that we have to accept its moral limitations. Sometimes the tradition, as in the case of the acceptance of slavery, has to be evaluated and changed. This critical stance toward tradition can also be seen in the difference between a tradition based on love and one derived from force.

We have to ask what of the past is adequate to engage the present and how this is in continuity with the core values of our faith.

The *Christian tradition* is rooted in unmerited love and is fundamentally oriented toward peace. It may be contrasted with a tradition of domination that reaches back to the early Babylonian myth of creation and finds its modern expression in the myth of redemptive violence that dominates contemporary movies, television, and many sports. The way of love is the path of nonviolence, rooted in the self-emptying compassion of Jesus Christ on the cross. This path leads beyond conflict to mutuality.[25] The Christian church has not always lived out this tradition consistently. Still, it sees in the Sermon on the Mount an invitation to strive toward a vision of God's ultimate restoration of this planet and human history. So we have to ask what of the past is adequate to engage the present and how this is in continuity with the core values of our faith.

Tradition and the Case of Domestic Violence

To live the way of Jesus is to embody an ethic of peace over against one of pervasive violence. When the issue is domestic violence, Shawn Copeland does not believe the church has been living what it proclaims. "What is so very troubling about violence in the United States...is that it is no longer shocking. Violence has subjugated our imaginations." Churches demonstrate considerable ambivalence toward violence. Their tradition espouses nonviolence as a means of achieving social justice. Yet they tend to follow the conventions of societal conflict by tolerating or sanctioning military conflict between nations while advocating the opposite when it comes to domestic personal relationships. The most vulnerable are enjoined to submit meekly to brutality, even in the name of the suffering of Jesus Christ. What is significant for understanding violence in such a society is a culture formed by meanings and values that shape imagination. Spiritual freedom and moral responsibility are exchanged for economic psychic security.[26] A consumerist, hedonistic culture easily spawns alienation, self-hatred, and violence. Rap music powerfully reflects this reality. The film industry bathes violence in a surreal light, making it excessive, gratuitous, strangely compelling, and roughly erotic. Modern films interweave pleasure, pressure, and pain. The film *Boys Don't Cry* is a sickening exposure of depraved brutality against a love-starved transvestite young woman. Not realizing beforehand just what the movie was about, I found myself so numbed by its raw, dehumanizing abusiveness that I didn't know how to react. Violence leaves us discouraged and dispirited. We leave such films culturally wounded and spiritually and morally flayed.

> *Because violence in our culture is deeply rooted in our inherited traditions, the sermon needs to build on an alternative tradition of the dignity of all persons.*

Because some of the causes of violence "lie in our internalization of the dislocations and value disorientations of wider U.S. [and Canadian] cultural and social matrices," the sermon needs to build an alternative tradition. Thinking primarily of sermons from the African American tradition, Copeland speaks about "*drawing out* the centuries-old history of African Americans," including images and symbols that draw on the "soul-field" of black culture. Theologically, the sermon needs to project a vision of God's ultimate future that jettisons the aesthetics of submission and restores the full dignity and value of all human persons. Every woman and every person of color needs to be assured that the gospel demands their full participation in a humanity recreated in God's image. In proclaiming God's self-giving love, preaching calls the church to pour itself out with genuine risk and compassion to end violence in whatever way it can.[27] Re-traditionalizing is not merely an intellectual process but an empowering vision that leads to moral action. Appealing to tradition is itself a way of living into a tradition.[28]

Ethics and the Authority of Scripture

We have been trying to discern *to what are we appealing when we express our viewpoints*. We have focused on experience, reason, and tradition. We now turn to scripture because preaching constantly appeals to the authority of scripture. In every chapter we have referred repeatedly to specific biblical passages and in some cases (for example, Gal. 5; Ex. 20; and Mt. 5–7) have engaged in more extended discussion of them. In leaving this authoritative source for ethics to the last, we have tried to make sure that the other three sources of authority are taken with utmost seriousness. Scripture's role has been central in the history of preaching, as I believe it should be. Scripture's dominating position may, however, eliminate the other sources of authority by default. We may fail to bring experience, reason, and tradition to the Bible with the kind of vigor that truly respects the voice of scripture in rigorous ethical dialogue. The Bible is quite capable of being engaged on the basis of our other sources of authority.

Again, we emphasize that the history of preaching has long been understood primarily as a proclamation of the word of God. That *Word*, to be sure, is Christ. Yet the incarnate Christ is known through scripture. So what does it mean to appeal to the authority of the Bible? We have three tasks:

1. **to explore more directly various presumptions** about the authority of the Bible and draw out what at least some of this means for preaching;

2. **to introduce what is involved in the interpretation** of biblical texts. Recently, denominations have made the interpretation of homosexuality a test case for the authority of scripture. We illustrate appeals to scripture with this moral

question. How preachers use scripture when dealing with controversial issues gives listeners a clear indication of how their pastor really understands biblical authority; and
3. to discuss the interrelationship between experience, reason, tradition, and scripture.

The Authority of Scripture Per Se

Because the church's debates about the authority of the Bible are so vast and intense, we will focus on two matters: salient facets of biblical authority and the meaning of *the word of God.*

1. Salient facets of biblical authority.[29] A number of facets of the authority of scripture help us understand some aspects of this library of ancient texts for the life of the church.

- The Bible is a complex book composed by many different writers with an **identifiable core,** namely, that God, our Creator, is also our Redeemer and will bring creation to completion. To take this collection seriously is to recognize its central thrust while acknowledging its constant strangeness and continuing surprises.
- The Bible does not interpret itself. **Interpretation** is a complex task in which we may be tempted to substitute what we want the Bible to say for its own witness to God.
- Interpretation involves **imagination** so that we can join the movement of the text beyond itself and gain fresh insight, but such insight does not carry the weight of absoluteness.
- We cannot engage the text without **vested interests** and therefore tend to read a part of the text as though it is the whole text. We admit, therefore, that we have a propensity to distort the text to meet our own needs. One way we may help overcome this tendency is by reading the Bible in community, thus learning to listen to it ecumenically and encouraging open reflection on what the text is saying.
- Sometimes **the Spirit inspires** our understanding of the Bible, and we are moved by this experience in ways that are wonderfully, enigmatically insightful. We dare not presume this inspiration but can rejoice when we believe it happens.
- The Bible's authority is **empowering.** It is not so much power over as power for. In giving us access to the gospel, the Bible releases us to live beyond the confines of our broken world and invites us toward God's alternative reality in Christ. But

because this reality is God's, we dare not seek to manage it or to claim it as a tool with which to win our moral debates.

2. The word of God—metaphor and witness to truth.[30] When we say that the Bible—as a collection of writings by human beings—is *the word of God,* we are speaking figuratively. Because God is spirit (Jn. 4:24), God does not literally write or literally speak. This does not mean that God may not communicate with us in a direct way. The Spirit can influence us profoundly in ways that are quite mysterious but feel very real. Yet the expression "the word of God" is a metaphor joining a human activity—using words—with something divine. A metaphor is an enriched form of speech expressing meaning beyond what is literal. This metaphor ("the Bible is the word of God") expresses God's self-disclosure through conversation. Human language can be both beautiful and singularly limited. For example, words between conversation partners who love each other seek to express their inner selves. Such communication is often frustratingly inadequate; it never quite says it all. In the case of scripture, the people of Israel perceived God's self-disclosure in Torah, in prophetic speech, and in the words of the sages. Christians perceive this disclosure additionally in Jesus of Nazareth. The Bible as a verbal form of this symbolic Word is a witness to God and to Jesus Christ.

> *When we say that the Bible is "the word of God," we are speaking metaphorically, joining the human activity of using words with something divine.*

When this testimony is *inscripturated,* it moves beyond its originally intended meaning (like all written texts), moves beyond the confines of its original setting, and has the capacity to refer to something more than it did at first. As a result it continues to speak. In the case of scripture, God can disclose God's self in new ways to engage us in our time and in our situations. So there is a mutual transformation of the text and of the reader as Christians discern their call to discipleship by the same Spirit at work in the early church. All of this is an interpretive task in response to the text's witness as word of God.

The term *witness* is drawn from law courts seeking to discover "the truth" through the testimony given at a trial. The testimony of such witnesses is always partial, perspectival, and open to error. When the gospel of John refers repeatedly to *witness* and asserts the truthfulness of *witnesses* (from Jesus to John the Baptist to the Beloved

Disciple and to the latter's community), it is a claim of faith seeking understanding. The fact that the very nature of testimony is partial and provisional does not mean that it cannot claim to be true.

How do we appropriate this testimony? Jesus says, "Anyone who resolves to do the will of God will know whether the teaching is from God or whether I am speaking on my own" (Jn. 7:17). We affirm the truth that *the Bible is the word of God* by participating in the story and living in its community of suffering love. This does not end the interpretive struggle, but it reorients the interpreter to read within the tradition of scripture itself.[31] Preaching as witness to Jesus Christ is an attempt to follow the example of the biblical witnesses. As those who point listeners to Christ, preachers also bear witness to the authority of scripture in its testimony as reliable witness.

Preaching That Engages Biblical Interpretation

Taking an ancient sacred text seriously as an integral part of preaching involves interpretation. The words on the pages of scripture are often very different from everyday speech; the stories and injunctions, the poetry and imagery, and the historical allusions are increasingly unfamiliar and confusing to many seated in the pews. It seems increasingly difficult for many preachers to know just what their listeners know or understand of a given biblical story or reference. How do we get from scripture to present-day understanding in ways that reflect responsible interpretation? This becomes even more difficult when trying to engage as difficult an issue as homosexual practice. A four-stage process outlined by Richard Hays in *The Moral Vision of the New Testament* guides us.[32]

The process of interpretation includes discovering what the biblical text says, paying attention to its relation to biblical themes, reading it imaginatively about ourselves, and letting it empower our discipleship.

---

1. Description. What does this particular text say? What is distinctive about this writer and this writing? What is the form of the text? What symbolic world is evident in its language? Our problem with biblical texts, says William Willimon, is not "that we are modern, critical and skeptical whereas the text is naïve, primitive, and credulous." Rather, the text is too *thick,* too opaque. It is not the fault of the text if modern people "live by epistemologies too limited to enable them to hear the text." We may try so hard to get *the* right reading that we violate the text itself.[33] Quoting a text without really understanding it against its historical and cultural setting is not an appeal to authority but an expression of authoritarian reductionism. Such action represents a pragmatic utilitarian disregard for what the text may actually be saying. As noted earlier, how preachers deal with texts does not go unnoticed by congregations, even when the latter do not go through a deliberate process of analyzing this matter. So we listen for what scripture texts say about homosexual behavior. Leviticus 18:22 is a legal text that prohibits male homosexual intercourse to preserve a purity of patrilineal descent,[34] or because it appears to threaten the very "stuff" of life.[35] Romans 1:18–32 draws on Genesis 1–2 and views homosexual acts as contrary to the intentions of the Creator.[36] But Paul also says that whoever judges others will also be judged (Rom. 2:1).

2. Reading in context. Interpretation requires attention to the larger context of the canon of scripture. We have already noted the flexibility of the tradition in the biblical trajectory of covenant. Homosexuality is also part of the larger trajectory of human sexuality in which marriage, divorce, prostitution, gender differentiation, and homosexuality are viewed from the perspective of the polarity of male and female in Genesis 1–2.[37] But other commentators note the cultural contingency of the creation stories and stress the biblical trajectory of justice-love.[38] Some would say that we should acknowledge biblical diversity and leave it at that, but Hays believes we should try to discern coherence based on the images of community, cross, and new creation.[39] Our preaching needs to move beyond selected textual fragments to help congregations see the larger picture that frames a given text.

3. Appropriating the biblical text today. One of the primary arguments in recent homosexuality debates is that the Bible's view of homosexuality is so different from what we understand today that we must at least be cautious about its normative authority.[40] How, then, do we *appropriate* scripture?[41] Appropriating the text involves an imaginative re-reading; it means "living with the text in such a way that we come to experience the story as fundamentally about us."[42] The church is a community of interpretation seeking to "indwell" the biblical story rather than accommodate it to contemporary culture. It does so in order to discern itself as a community of mutual care within which those who are most vulnerable (including homosexual persons) can feel secure in Christ.[43]

4. Embodying the biblical text in the life of the church. Interpretation is not complete until we begin to live it. Appeals to the authority of scripture mean little if we do not evidence its empowerment in our discipleship. "*Obedient interpretation*...is to see how the Bible authorizes, evokes, and permits a world that is an alternative to the deathly world of our dominant value system."[44] This calls for interpretive obedience. Depending on how one draws conclusions from the previous three sections, practical implications can be imagined from advocating the civil rights of homosexual persons in society, to the welcoming of such persons into the fellowship of the church, to same-sex blessings or the requirement that gay persons remain celibate, to ordaining practicing homosexual persons.[45] This step reopens the larger question on the relationship between the various authorities that we have been exploring in this chapter.

Ethics and the Interrelationship of Authority Sources

A significant issue for preaching is the interrelationship and relative weight among experience, reason, tradition, and scripture. Denominational studies on sexuality frequently make scripture primary, but the division between majority and minority reports reveals variations in ordering or at least an unwillingness to give primacy to scripture.[46] For example, Roman Catholics often emphasize tradition, and some liberationist theologies stress experience.[47] Anderson argues that if one recognizes Jesus as God's definitive revelation, scripture becomes primary because "it is indispensable for understanding Jesus as the Christ."[48] Cahill, on the other hand, uses the four sources of authority as mutually corrective of one another.[49] Sometimes the relative weight given to a particular authority depends on the issue being discussed. More attention was focused on reason or scientific studies in the human genome project and in the two legal cases. Approaches to poverty and welfare reflected differing traditions. The church's view of God's providence was significant in our evaluation of legalized gambling. Frequently, biblical passages came to the fore. These authorities are not mutually exclusive but complementary and imaginatively suggestive for preaching.

If one recognizes Jesus as God's definitive revelation, scripture becomes primary because "it is indispensable for understanding Jesus as the Christ."

The preacher, then, clarifies how a given sermon is authorized and whether or not this is made explicit. Over time congregations "get a feel" for how experience, reason, tradition, and scripture are valued. Still, they could find it helpful in some sermons, at least, to know which authority is being appealed to and why. The more controversial the subject matter, the more transparent appeals to authority would seem to be necessary. But the key purpose of such specificity is to ensure that the sermon assists the congregation to become engaged by God's will, purpose, and enabling presence. Often this can be accomplished through relating an experience; sometimes it turns on an explanation of some data. The church's recognition of a failure in its tradition may illuminate a rereading of biblical passages (for example, on slavery). Of course, a biblical vision such as that of jubilee can open up fresh discussion about how we reason or what we have accepted as part of our tradition. Whatever decisions we make ought to advance the ethical responsibility of the sermon for the challenge, nurture, and doxology of the church.

We have now come to the end of our examination of the six areas on our interconnected ethical web for preaching. Preacher, preaching, and congregation have constantly been woven through our discussion. We look now at the preacher as proclaimer of ethics, the sermon as ethical communication, and the congregation as ethical community.

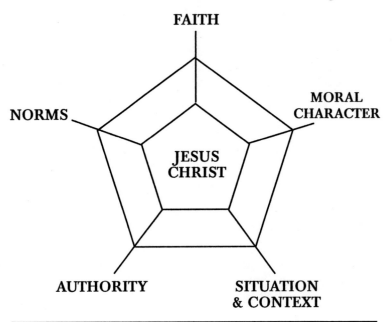

7

PREACHER, SERMON, AND CONGREGATION

Preacher as Proclaimer of Ethics, Sermon as Ethical Communication, and Congregation as Ethical Community

Previous chapters have sought to integrate preaching and moral engagement by clarifying five aspects of moral reflection: (1) studying faith convictions, (2) understanding moral character, (3) articulating moral norms, (4) examining particular situations and contexts and (5) appealing to specific authorities, especially the authority of scripture. All of these have revolved around the common center of the web, Jesus Christ, who is at the heart of both our proclamation and our ethics. This sequential journey has allowed us to focus on each aspect of ethical reflection, always seeking to reference our exploration to the act of preaching.

We stated in chapter 1 that this ethical web is a heuristic device to help us develop a comprehensive approach to preaching and ethics. We set the web's elements out as five areas to facilitate the gradual appropriation of this method. Because the web is interconnected, one begins to see how each area impacts the others. This also means that in a given sermon one could begin at any point on the web. We could start with a particular situation or with a question about moral character. We might acknowledge early on how and why we are appealing to a given authority. We may introduce a sermon with a certain normative statement or ethical principle and show how it is connected with what we believe. There is no "right" formula or technique here, just a calling to faithful proclamation.

So preachers may begin using this method by concentrating on one chapter at a time, moving from faith or theology to appeals to authority. In the process they will inevitably reflect on themselves as proclaimers of ethics. They will also keep on exploring both the sermon as ethical communication and the congregation as an ethical community. In doing so, we assume that the overall goal of preaching is to inspire, nurture, and enable the church to be and act as those who are baptized into a new way of living in a secular world. The ethical purpose of sermons is to empower God's people to engage the moral life in faithfulness to Jesus Christ.

The Preacher as Proclaimer of Ethics

The preacher's role in ethics is more than developing a capacity to learn and use the discipline of ethics. Certainly, increasing one's ability to employ moral reasoning is important, but so are the person and authority of the preacher. What is the relationship between who the preacher is as a moral person and the act of preaching? What is the ethical effect of the way we view the authority of the preacher?

The Person, Character, and Spirituality of the Preacher

Preachers ultimately stand before God. Fred Craddock's wonderful imagery about sermon preparation is especially helpful.

To assume that the sheer weight of the authority of the sacred texts, the faithful commitment of a regular congregation, and the inspiration of a worship setting will sustain the pulpit without the preacher's own wrestling with the question of what it is we are doing is serious error. The emptiness at the center of such a ministry will have its hollow echo in the soul of the one who preaches, and that echo will not pass the ear of the church unnoticed.

In light of this observation, Craddock discusses the process of spiritual preparation and communication of the sermon in terms of three striking phrases: "proceeding from silence, heard in a whisper, shouted from the housetop."[1] The preacher as proclaimer of ethics has to stand in the silence of receptivity, listen with deep attentiveness to the whisper of God, and be willing to shout the insights of the Spirit with passionate conviction.

IMITATE ME

The apostle Paul confessed, "We do not proclaim ourselves; we proclaim Jesus Christ as Lord and ourselves as your slaves for Jesus' sake" (2 Cor. 4:5). Elsewhere he urged, "Brothers and sisters, join in imitating me" (Phil. 3:17). We face a dialectic here, not a contradiction. When he called a church to imitate him, Paul placed "himself squarely within the moral and pedagogical tradition that assumed that a teacher is one who is willing to be exposed to the imitative glare of a student." For him, "teachers have a responsibility to live as they teach, to walk as they speak." Listeners "are challenged not only to know about some things but to be transformed by someone."[2]

As Jesus embodied his own proclamation in his life, death, and resurrection, those who preach Christ seek to live by Paul's remarkable confession: "It is no longer I who live, but it is Christ who lives in me" (Gal. 2:20). Preachers do not live by a different standard from the rest of the church. Moral character is the same for all. But if preachers are to call others to follow Christ, they must strive through receptivity and attentiveness to be what they preach.

> ***Preachers seeking to proclaim the gospel of Christ and call the church to follow him must themselves be what they preach.***

In our chapter on moral character we saw how who we are is the bridge between what we believe and what we are to do. In a culture that emphasizes the ability to communicate effectively, believability has become more important than being truthful. Honesty and integrity are not valued as much as being convincing. Preachers live in the competitive matrix that breeds this attitude. They feel the pressure to convince because of the voluntaristic nature of the church. Constantly having their church compared statistically to other churches, they can begin to substitute communicational techniques for faithfulness to the gospel. They may also be tempted by the thousands of sermons offered through the Internet to take shortcuts in sermon preparation. If they abdicate their responsibilities, they undermine their integrity; and congregations are not fooled. Listeners know when the sermon has been created out of a deep experience of a text, listened to on behalf of themselves as God's people, and pondered in terms of how the gospel should be lived.[3]

Genuine involvement with people and clear interpretation of moral awareness can be utterly transforming. Several years ago, I was with a group of North Americans in Sao Paulo, Brazil, to meet with the renowned educator Paulo Freire. We were about to begin our conversation with Freire when two maids came in to serve us demitasses of coffee. One of them began by offering coffee to Freire. He immediately stopped talking to us and engaged her in a brief, animated conversation (in Portuguese). When he finished, he turned to us and explained that he had asked her how things were going with her and her family. He then went on to say that he believed everyone who offers this or any other kind of service deserves to be recognized and treated as a human being. That simple experience changed the way I saw people and inspired me to be more attentive to every person I meet as an individual person, no matter what business they are in or how they are relating to me at the moment. I was changed by what he did out of who he was.

THE CALL TO BE SPIRITUAL

To embody ethics, as already noted, is something profoundly spiritual. Will Campbell speaks of his calling to be a preacher as "surrendering to preach."[4] Spiritual struggle arises from the experience of being pulled in many different directions. Some in the church see pastors primarily as chaplains to meet their personal needs. Preachers may feel inclined to emphasize the pastoral dimension of their ministry and neglect the prophetic call of the gospel. At other times, preachers feel the pull of the prophetic word and forget that it needs to be offered with pastoral sensitivity if people are to discover the transforming power of grace. Pastoral and prophetic need each other.[5] Some want sermons that give clear and definite answers to their moral questions or that interpret biblical texts with simple clarity. Others expect preachers to acknowledge the limits of their research and to admit clearly the subjective dimensions of their interpretations.[6] Often these kinds of tensions are not made explicit but are felt nevertheless. In the tautness of the discernment process, the preacher knows that being ethical is very personal and deeply spiritual.

Preachers, like everyone else, are susceptible to larger spiritual forces and are called to evidence in their own persons a spirituality of nonviolent resistance.

But the spiritual issue is much larger. If, as we have indicated repeatedly in earlier chapters, the dimensions of evil are more clearly revealed by the principalities and powers, preachers must recognize that they, too, are susceptible to them. They, too, need to resist them in what can best be called "a spirituality of nonviolent resistance."[7]

This means that in their sermons preachers do not dodge the systemic dimensions of evil signaled in the biblical text. Rather, they seek to help congregations connect such matters as interpersonal conflicts with larger forces at work.[8]

The Preacher's Authority

The preacher's ethical example may be inspiring to the congregation, but the role of the preacher as an ethical model in society has changed over time. When the church had a recognized public role, clergy could be a moral force in society. With the disestablishment of the church, their influence has been reduced to the personal and private sphere. Congregations have become voluntary associations, and clergy are expected to be an influence in attracting people to their sanctuaries. As a result, says Martin Marty, ministers are "on their own" and are no longer under external norms.[9]

To speak of the authority of the preacher moves against the erosion of authority in many aspects of modern Western societies over the last forty years. Christopher Lasch draws attention to the diminishment of social expectations and the abdication of authority. In schools, businesses, and law courts, "authorities conceal their power behind a façade of benevolence."[10] Instead of being appropriately challenged to make tough moral decisions, people retreat into a self-absorption that cuts off concern for others and leaves each alone and lonely.

This has affected churches and preaching. Fred Craddock noted an increasing tentativeness on the part of preachers ministering in the late 1960s. "Rarely, if ever, in the history of the church have so many firm periods slumped into commas and so many triumphant exclamation points curled into question marks." This internal reluctance to speak with clarity and boldness is consistent with the external attitude of the congregation. No longer, adds Craddock, can preachers presuppose a general recognition of their authority as clergy. They cannot assume that others recognize the authority of the church or even the authority of scripture.[11] But the issue is not the authority of preaching as such but the nature of that authority. In my view, it has been unfortunate to speak of the preacher "as one without authority." Craddock himself clarifies the problem as "the authoritarian foundation of traditional preaching." Such authoritarian preaching was based on a passive-receptive stance of the congregation rather than an active participatory one. Craddock really wanted to inspire responsible biblical preaching as "the awesome burden of interpreting scripture *for the congregation to which one preaches.*" Such preaching demands rare courage as the preacher stands between the biblical text and the situation faced by the congregation at that moment. In the process the "congregation is born in preaching," and preaching "is born in the congregation."[12] The work of the Spirit in preacher, congregation, and the Word is the dynamic force empowering the sermon for transformation.

The cultural shift in the sixties that helped push these insights to the surface was also evident in the concomitant women's movement. Through the following decades Christian feminist scholars clarified their understanding of authority as "a quality of presence, mutuality, and integrity" and a "humanness that is so persuasive and honest that it calls people into connection and solidarity." Authority is not "set-apartness." Rather, authority is woven together with intimacy so that power and empowerment are connected. The effect on preaching was greater emphasis on the authority of experience, both of the preacher and of the congregation.[13] Indeed, the so-called new homiletic that developed focused on creating an experience in the lives of the listening, participating congregation. But is this a sign of an entertainment culture in which congregations simply want the sermon to be "an *experience* that moves them?"[14]

In a way, David Greenhaw both challenges Craddock's formulation and builds on the participatory role of the congregation when he argues that the "gospel cannot be proclaimed without authority." Preaching necessarily articulates claims on our lives and announces the newness of what God is doing. While "the text has something to say," transformation happens "only when the congregation takes up the interpretive work," when the people "speak the gospel in their own lives." The interpretive task for Greenhaw includes a *conceptual process* without which the congregation cannot make the connections between the text, the sermon, and their own lives.[15] Authority so construed implies an important role for reason and sees the ethics of the sermon in the discipleship of God's people together and scattered in the world.

Tom Long uses the analogy of a law-court witness as the central image for preaching. He sees in this image a new way of emphasizing the authority of the preacher. This authority rests "not on rank or power" but on "what the preacher has seen and heard." The congregation sets the preacher apart with the authority of ordination as a sworn witness to the truth of God's promise and claim.[16] The pulpit is not a place for the preacher to propound his or her personal ideas or agenda, tempting as this may be. Nor do preachers lord it over their listeners. They stand under the discipline of the Word that witnesses to Christ.[17] Indeed, preachers ultimately "embrace a strange kind of powerlessness, like the powerlessness of Jesus on the cross. They finally must rely on God to make effective...the practice of preaching itself."[18]

> *The preacher as witness to Jesus Christ embraces the powerlessness of the cross and knows that ultimately only God makes proclamation effective.*

The Sermon as Ethical Communication

A central question in previous chapters concerns the relationship between the biblical text and ethical exploration. At issue also are the scope, potential, and limitations of the sermon in communicating ethics. We now reflect further on these and what is at the heart and center of preaching that makes it an empowering means of ethical discovery and inspiration for discipleship.

Preaching on Biblical Texts and Ethics

Because scripture is the primary witness to Jesus Christ, who is central in our preaching, the importance of taking biblical texts seriously is assumed. In our ethical web we have approached the development of ethical awareness by drawing on our biblical (and theological) heritage both to form faith as the basis of Christian ethics and to clarify how the community of the baptized is to manifest moral character. We began our consideration of moral obligations with specific normative statements: the Ten Commandments and the Sermon on the Mount. Careful attention to biblical texts—even when explicit reference to ethics is not made in the sermon—should not be underestimated in shaping the understanding and life of the church as an ethical community.

> *Scripture informs our faith, shapes moral character, clarifies our obligations, and helps us grapple with complex ethical issues.*

Congregations need and often hope for specific help in working out the ethical implications of a given text or theological theme. Frequently, a particular moral question arises from the biblical text. In response to those who criticized him for allowing someone to anoint his head with expensive oil, Jesus said, "For you always have the poor with you" (Mt. 26:11). This statement refers back to the Sabbath Year tradition in which the reality of perpetual need calls for opening one's hand "to the poor and needy" (Deut. 15:11).[19] The text so interpreted invites the preacher to elaborate specific ways in which this response to poverty is a moral obligation. This may be through a story; it could include some analysis of what leads to poverty and how churches have responded. It could even venture into the realm of politics to encourage the congregation to relate their understanding of faith to the larger world. The challenge would be to enable the congregation to see how their concrete ethical reflection on poverty arises from the text and its witness to Christ. A sermon on the anointing of Jesus would make explicit how his statement about the poor relates to this incident. To give the impression that in this gospel story Jesus disparages the poor on this occasion would, of course, be unethical in light of the source of this saying about them.

Although the tradition of preaching from biblical texts may be the dominant one, David Buttrick thinks that it has been overstressed.[20] He is among a number of people[21] who see a place for the interpretation of the human situation in the tradition of the topical sermon. The topical sermon can and often does use biblical texts, but these arise from the ethical issue being explored. A sermon on a large moral theme such as the ethics of genetic research can open up ways of thinking about our created nature and could be very helpful in probing the limits of knowledge as reflected in the prohibition to eat from the tree of the knowledge of good and evil in Genesis 3.[22] The danger, of course, is that the sermon can too easily reflect the personal opinions of the preacher without the underlying authority of scripture.

The preacher may use other creative possibilities. A sermon on capital punishment, for instance, could explore the ways in which people with opposing views on this subject have used the Bible to support their own positions. Textual preaching (sometimes too limited by the lectionary selections of a given Sunday) often does not allow for this wider biblical exploration of complex themes.[23] Preaching on a specific moral theme could be very helpful from time to time as long as the thrust of the sermon sends people back to their discipleship in Christ. The Spirit is also at work in the world and may draw our attention to something out there as the starting point for sermonic reflection.

The Scope, Ethical Potential, and Limits of Preaching

What can one sermon do? Sometimes a lot, sometimes not as much as we might like. I heard a sermon on the parable of the talents (Mt. 25:14–30) in a Pentecostal congregation in a very poor area just outside of San Jose, Costa Rica. The preacher claimed that the harsh words of Jesus in damning the servant with one talent were intended to shock his listeners out of complacency and into responsibility. This is the only sermon I have encountered on this text that did not avoid this final verse about judgment.[24] Congregations gradually notice what parts of a text we draw on and what we avoid. They get a sense of our boldness or our timidity.

Sermons, naturally, also have their limits. The process of ethical reflection requires asking more than can be pursued in a sermon. Don Browning, for instance, asks five reflective questions.

1. What **theological images** or symbols can assist us in addressing a given problem?
2. What **human need** is implicit in this issue?
3. How **has the church responded** to this sort of problem in the past, and how should it respond today?
4. How are **we able to respond** now?
5. What **strategy** should we follow?

These questions assume issues of theology, obligations, tradition, context, roles, and rules.[25] They require time, collective research, discussion, decision-making structures, and so on.[26] In the midst of these questions and ways of engaging ethics, what distinctive part do sermons play?

The possible contribution of preaching becomes clearer when we ask about which of a variety of outcomes a given sermon might have. Each of the following is worthy of consideration:

- calling the congregation to *faith*—engendering in them a perspective of God's creating, sustaining, and redeeming activity that provides a moral vision and an ability to see the world in relation to God;
- inspiring and inculcating *moral character*—elucidating those habits of the heart that are characteristic of Christian discipleship;
- rehearsing and teaching moral *norms*—clarifying God's requirements, inculcating values, and setting forth moral claims to assist listeners to live out their discipleship;
- encouraging congregations to probe the *situation and context* of particular moral issues; and
- lifting up and identifying the sources of moral *authority*—helping

congregations evaluate that to which they appeal in making moral decisions.

(The various participles chosen above are deliberate and varied to suggest how each aspect of preaching might be shared in a sermon.)

As implied already, the various aspects of ethical formation cannot be dealt with in every sermon. One of our problems in preaching is thinking that we have to say it all at once. Preaching, however, was never meant to be a one-shot deal. Individual sermons are part of a larger whole just as readings assigned for a given Sunday have to be viewed with the whole Christian year in mind. One aspect of a moral question can be raised in one sermon, and another on the same theme in another sermon. Sometimes the best we can do is open up a theme or problem and invite people who want to explore it further to gather for a discussion or join a study group. The analytic process used in chapter 5 cannot be fully spelled out in a sermon, but aspects of it can. Similarly, the fourfold interpretive method for looking at biblical texts in chapter 6 is essential, in my view, for grasping the moral vision of the Bible, but they do not always need to be made completely explicit in a given sermon.

Homiletical openings and closings bear particular scrutiny given the limits noted above. At the beginning, the sermon should clarify where the congregation is being invited to travel and what sort of ethical call the gospel compels. When the sermon moves to its close, it should facilitate ethical response: a new perspective, some expression of discipleship, a willingness to probe an issue further. This means it may need to end on a minor key, as though the sermon is unfinished or off-key. Preference for a more settled major key could be a sign of capitulation to bland, equivocal niceness. A hard-hitting television exposé of Enron's collapse[27] lost most of its impact because after describing the disaster, it related how all the middle-management types in the company eventually landed on their feet. The viewer quickly forgets the thousands of people whose pensions were eviscerated in this evil misadventure.

The beginning of the sermon should clarify what sort of ethical call the gospel compels, and its closing should facilitate ethical response.

The scope, potential, and limits of the sermon as ethical communication are a matter of judgment—of course, one of prayerful judgment. Sometimes this requires more than our courage or reason permits, and sometimes less than our zeal or intuition tries to attempt.

The Heart and Center of Ethical Preaching

The apostle Paul made two statements about preaching that get at the very heart of the sermon as ethical communication. The first is "I decided to know nothing among you except Jesus Christ, and him crucified"; the second is, "My speech and my proclamation were not with plausible words of wisdom, but with a demonstration of the Spirit and of power" (1 Cor. 2:2, 4). The cross is at the center of Christian preaching because there God embraces humanity in a space-creating act of self-giving that forever changes ethics. In this act the demonic power of evil is revealed; here, the power of life finally triumphs over death.[28] At the cross we are given what James Kay calls "a bifocal vision" of reality. We see ourselves through the lens of near vision, enslaved by the world as it is, and through the lens of far vision, invaded by God's new creation in Christ.[29] We see the powers of the world in their fallenness, and also the world as it will be transformed by Christ. The lordship of Christ at the core of preaching ethics[30] is most fully revealed in his dying and rising, where the world-to-come has already been inaugurated. The church that allows itself to be formed by the grace of the crucified Christ in openness to the other becomes "a sacrament of God in the world" and can free culture from its psychic and physical destructiveness.[31]

> *The cross is at the center of Christian preaching because there God embraces humanity in a space-creating act of self-giving that forever changes ethics.*

Paul's second observation acknowledged that the real power of preaching comes from the Spirit. Later in the chapter he clarified this by noting that the Spirit connects us with the deep things of God and gives us the very mind of Christ (1 Cor. 2:10, 16). In commenting on the work of the Spirit in the church, Michael Welker says that the Spirit's power is reflected "in every good sermon" and enables understanding that leads to commonality across vast diversities. In the outpouring of the Spirit at Pentecost, "God is at work in this ruptured world." The cardinal virtues of faith, hope, and love enable us to discover "the force fields of the Spirit" in such a way that human contacts, understanding, attentiveness, and self-withdrawal (in the sense of self-giving) are possible "in the Spirit."[32] This is strange, compelling language that links the work of the Spirit to preaching, so that one feels that the church is empowered to live its ethical obligations and reflect the freedom of the gospel.

The Congregation as Ethical Community

We have assumed throughout this volume that the congregation participates in the sermon. Preaching ethics requires the involvement of the church as a people who seek to live their faith. We will explore what this implies and then clarify further the various ways in which the congregation is engaged in the event of preaching. Finally, we will speak of the congregation as herald and servant of the Word in the world.

The Congregation as a People Who Seek to Live Their Faith

The congregation as a community of people shapes the experience of preaching as much as the preacher. Their receptivity to the gospel can be felt both by the preacher and by one another as they listen. On one occasion when Jesus' listeners resisted his message, "he could do no deed of power there" and "was amazed at their unbelief" (Mk. 6:5, 6). On the other hand, the Christians in Thessalonica were commended because when they received the word of God, they "accepted it not as a human word but as what it really is, God's word." The proclamation was accepted not only as God speaking but also as being "at work in you believers" (1 Thess. 2:13). This is an ethical comment. The church sought to live what it believed.

The congregation as a community of people shapes the experience of preaching as much as the preacher.

The congregation cannot hear the ethical import of the sermon if it is not disposed to live it or if its own behavior as a community contradicts what is being proclaimed. The way decisions are made, the inclusion or exclusion of certain voices in the congregation, the attitude toward people of different races, financial and other policies, and the difficulty of really sharing spiritual insight–any or all of these–can prevent the sermon from happening. By contrast, "where words of hope and freedom are read, where relationships of trust and faith can be experimented with, where moral inquiry and education can occur, where experiments of celebration and critique can happen," a church can become what Rebecca Chopp calls a *constitutive community*.[33] There are churches who evidence in their collective life that they are indeed called and *constituted* by Christ to be a transforming presence of freedom and hope for its members and for the world.

Recently, I was involved with a congregation trying to sort out its collective values. It was an inspiring afternoon as voices not always heard in the congregation shared their perspectives and others truly listened. A level of trust emerged through which collective discovery led to insight. In that community a group of people felt safe enough to be secure, and secure enough to imagine. They saw themselves both in their human vulnerability and as people of faith. They saw in their surrounding community an interactive possibility. They saw doxology and the service of the Word as drawing them and their neighbors together. They experienced truth, but would it be lived? Every time the congregation listens without expecting that the gospel makes a difference, the more the sermon is viewed as an exercise of low expectations. To the extent, however, that the congregation lives out of its newly expressed vision, the preaching of the Word will lead them further as an ethical community.

Congregational Participation in Preaching

It follows that a congregation that seeks to live its faith will listen to preaching with the expectation that the sermon can and should make a difference. This difference has to do not only with their collective life but also with their lives when they are scattered during the week. People sitting in the pew Sunday by Sunday more often than not want to make connections between the sermon and their daily engagement in work, study, or play. They want to grapple with how they are called to live their vocations as workers, families, and citizens. People "who yearn to have their lives shaped and characterized by the intrusion of God" intentionally bring their lives to the hearing of the Word and expect this hearing to make an ethical difference.[34]

> *When listeners yearn to have their lives intruded on by God, they intentionally bring them to the hearing of the Word and expect this hearing to make an ethical difference.*

For the sermon to live in its everyday world, the congregation must be invited to participate. "The ethics of the Word...begins with the ethics of conversation." If, says Brownsberger, pastors don't know enough about business or economics or whatever, they can ask. The very act of asking may create openings for mutual learning. "To enter someone else's workday life is implicitly to be invited also into that person's theological life."[35] Sermon preparation requires deliberate research into the life of the congregation if it is to become a timely, ethical word.[36]

Earlier in this chapter we noted that the congregation that wishes to participate finds in the inductive sermon a form that allows the listener to journey with the sermon as an experience of discovery. In this process listeners may also feel that it is appropriate to give feedback or say something about how the sermon relates to their world. Marvelous examples, both affirming and challenging, are offered by ethicist Stanley Hauerwas on Will Willimon's sermons in *Preaching to Strangers*. In one comment, Hauerwas commends Willimon because his sermons oftentimes let listeners make the connections by not saying things explicitly, "because when you say it explicitly, it cannot be known by the [listener] in the way necessary to be known truthfully." This is why stories "are so crucial for the sermon, because the story doesn't say–it shows."[37] Congregations may need to be given more permission than they ordinarily feel to do this. The mutual learning that could arise from such interactions would likely surprise both preacher and congregation. In the end, however, the potential for sermons to become ethical communication and the congregation to become an ethical community would be significantly enhanced.

Sermons are not finished when the preacher stops talking. They are meant to travel on in the lives of those who listen. Those who sit in the pews can wrestle with how this word proclaimed reveals the gospel of Christ and intentionally imagine how that gospel can take form in their lives. They hear the biblical story as fundamentally about them and for their journey now. We do not need so much to *apply* scripture to our lives as to *submit* our experience to its compelling and passionate anguish and hope. This needs to be corporate as well as individual. So we explore these matters as a community of the baptized who believe that the church is itself an integral part of the biblical drama and is guided by this drama into faithful ethical improvisation. The biblical text, like the sermon, continues to unfold.[38]

The Christian congregation at Corinth was told to herald the good news it had heard in Paul's preaching. They were like a letter to be read–a letter of Christ written by the Spirit on the tablets of their hearts (2 Cor. 3:2–3). A pastor in Kenya who has been repeatedly beaten by police for actively calling his government to end graft and corruption and effect democratic changes explains what keeps him going. "I live," he says, "by an eschatological vision as though the reality of what will be is already present."[39] Inspired by such a vision of God's alternative future, congregations are bound to become heralds of the gospel.

One Final Observation

Preacher, preaching, and congregation do not vie for importance; they need one another for the ethics of preaching to come alive. The proclaimer of ethics invites listeners to be transformed by the gospel in the very way that he or she seeks to be molded by that gospel. The sermon is a form of ethical communication that arises from careful biblical, theological, and ethical study for a specific community to appropriate in discerning its discipleship. The community of the baptized intends to live as an ethical community nurtured through the Word proclaimed by someone whom they have called as pastor, prophet, and preacher. As congregation and preacher open themselves to the transforming power of Jesus Christ, their horizons are expanded. They are connected beyond themselves to the source of ethics in the very being of God. Nothing could be more important in our interconnected ethical web for preaching than to put Jesus Christ at its center.

APPENDIX

AN ETHICAL SERMON ILLUSTRATED

Even a Judge Doesn't Have the Last Word

In the court drama *A Few Good Men,* a young, bright lawyer (played by Tom Cruise) is assigned to defend two marines accused of murdering another marine on the Guantanamo Naval Base in Cuba. Attempting to prepare a defense is a near impossible task because his star witness suddenly commits suicide and the base commander perpetually interferes. The lawyer is ready to quit, but his legal assistant gradually persuades him to persist. She even makes the audacious proposal of putting the base commander on the witness stand. Of course, the stakes are very high. If the lawyer loses, his own career is finished. Jack Nicholson, playing the role of the commander, is fiercely intimidating.

In the climactic final scene the commander arrogantly sneers at the whole system of justice, declaring himself to be above the law. In so doing he loses, and the lawyer and his clients win.

The justice system is also revealed as winning. But what if the court of law as such is corrupt? What if the judge hearing a case is a rogue who appropriates the law to himself or herself and fails to exercise justice? And what if that judge is confronted by a mere widow in a society in which women in general and widows in particular are almost nonpersons?

One thinks of the Nigerian woman Amina Lawal, who was raped and impregnated, and then blamed under Muslim Sharia and charged with adultery. She was then convicted and sentenced to die by a public stoning. There was, as could be expected, international outrage. But this was regarded in northern Nigeria as evidence of a decadent Western culture. The stoning was delayed until the child was born and weaned. Ultimately, the appeal process resulted in the woman's release. But she lived under the threat of a horrifying death for several years. Meanwhile, nothing is reported about the woman's male attacker.

The situation in the parable that Jesus tells is, on the surface, less dramatic but just as precarious. It is told not to rouse public opinion but to illuminate what God's kingdom is like—as over against the likes of the Guantanamo Naval Base and the exercise of Sharia. What lies behind the story appears to be a case of an inheritance dispute. A woman's husband dies, and a male member of the family takes her inheritance. She complains, but the family member apparently thinks he can get away with his theft by bribing the judge. The judge, in turn, keeps refusing to attend to the widow's complaint. This leaves her desperate in a society in which the welfare of women is dependent on male kinship relationships, including, in this case, the proceeds of her late husband's estate.

The Wisdom of Ben Sirach, an apocryphal writing from the early second century before Christ, contains a remarkable passage. Jesus was quite likely familiar with this passage. Following an admonition not to accept bribes, the ancient sage says, the Lord is judge and "will listen to the prayer of the one who is wronged. He will not ignore the supplication of the orphan, or the widow when she pours out her complaint...The prayer of the humble pierces the clouds, and it will not rest until it reaches its goal" (Sir. 35:16b–17, 21a).

This widow is a woman of prayer and knows that every person and every institution is ultimately accountable to God. This includes the judge who is called to fear God in order to execute justice. Indeed, God is the ultimate judge. In Exodus, the law required that widows be respected. Indeed, God is personally the defender and vindicator of widows and orphans. Elsewhere in Jewish tradition such cases were required to be heard before three judges, not just one, and were to be adjudicated without delay.

But here we have a corrupt judge who has no fear of God and no compassion for this human being who has come before him. Yet powerful as he is, he remains vulnerable. He is dependent on people coming to him for justice, and this, in turn, depends on his being

Appendix: An Ethical Sermon Illustrated   137

respected. This persistent widow is exposing his character as one who is not worthy of respect. If the public loses confidence in him as a judge, they will not come to him for his decisions, and he will be out of a job. As a result, she ends up being a threat to him, a threat that he likens to being pummeled incessantly as though in a boxing ring! He therefore decides to cut his losses and accedes to her request.

So we look again at the widow in this parable and see one who takes Torah teaching seriously and opens herself to God in prayer. As a result, she fights tenaciously for humanness. She has been living in the shadow of death, but now the blazing power of the revealing word of Torah ushers in life. She witnesses to the power of the resurrection over the tyranny of death.

This is not a moral tale about one person's persistence paying off. To individualize this as a contest of wits between two persons is to diminish the scope of the parable. This is a story about an institution—the justice system. This is what the Bible calls a principality, one created by God but operating as though it is independent of God. Many such principalities operate in the world. They include military operations, political parties, economic systems, international corporations, educational institutions, even churches. These loci of power are willed by God—not for their own ends but to serve the good of humanity and the rest of God's created order. According to the biblical witness, especially in the prophetic writings, the principalities are fallen and corruptible. They need to be called to account. So the parables of Jesus reveal what the order willed by God (what the evangelists refer to as the kingdom of God) looks like. They show what courts, businesses, nations, human relationships, and the like, ought to be like. The kingdom perspective invariably reverses power arrangements in a fallen world. In the words of the Magnificat: God brings down the powerful and lifts up the lowly (Lk. 1:52).

Such lively stories compel us to look at the storyteller—Jesus. Who is this person describing such a different view of the world? We are not so much invited to emulate the widow in the parable as to be attentive to the one who is the Word made flesh, who incarnates God's way. We listen to him as he teaches us in the Lord's Prayer to pray, "Your kingdom come. Your will be done, on earth as it is in heaven." The parable shows us that to pray for the coming of the kingdom is to challenge the principalities that dehumanize and destroy life—if not our own directly, then those of countless others whose position is akin to the widow in the parable. Jesus asks provocatively, "When the Son of Man comes, will he find faith on earth?" How is

God's reign evident here and now for those who are regarded as the least? This is the real test of the equity that is at the heart of biblical justice.

This parable is set within the larger context of the journey of the storyteller seen as a subverter. For in telling such stories, he is directly challenging the principalities, which are increasingly arrayed against him. He is finally betrayed, jailed, tried on trumped-up charges by an imposed foreign ruler, and crucified (even after being declared innocent). But death does not have the last word; the powers embodied in the Roman Empire finally crumble. Light dissipates darkness.

The evangelist Luke recorded this story for the church in the latter part of the first century c.e. Many Christians had been crucified, and the church was under constant threat throughout the empire. These first-century believers experienced being outcasts; they knew well the injustices of the legal system. As this gospel was first read, the listeners identified easily with the widow and recognized her courageous openness to God. They could feel the compassion of Jesus, who yielded his life on the cross to subvert the principalities. They were renewed in their own boldness to commit their way to God.

We ourselves, even in the relative tranquility of our Western democracies, sometimes feel overwhelmed by the threat of death, or at least by the limitation or denial of our humanness. We see war machines unleash their fury. We hear cries for peace being regarded as unpatriotic. We read of corporations collapsing because their financial accounting is corrupt while senior executives walk off with hundreds of millions of dollars; we understand that all the while this is happening, the pension funds of investors go up in smoke. When these and other signs of death surround us, we cling tenaciously to the parables of the kingdom of God, believing that the power of God is ultimately more powerful than the reign of death.

During the 1980s, Karen, a young woman from Winnipeg, and her friend from South America ended up doing mission work in war-torn El Salvador. They sought to help beleaguered peasants whose lives were flattened by overzealous police or cut down by death squads. Because of their association with such people, Karen and her friend were victimized. They suddenly found themselves jailed in a woman's prison, an even more sordid place of torture and death. Because Karen had a Canadian passport, however, the military police were reluctant to hold her. They released her and told her that she was free to leave. But she refused, saying they could not release her unless they also released her friend from South America. The guards stood astounded. Who would choose to stay in such a place, even for a friend? But Karen recognized that even such people are also victims of the militarized state, so she appealed to their hidden humanity. She pointed out to them that if any one of *them* were in trouble, they would go to the colleague's aid. The authorities agreed and allowed her friend to be released. When light shines in the darkness, the darkness cannot put it out. Even a judge does not have the last word.

This is the gospel of our Lord Jesus Christ.

Commentary

This sermon was written for *Preaching Word and Witness* (New Berlin, Wisc.: Liturgical Publications) for Proper 24, October 17, 2004, and I am grateful for permission to include this here. Since I was simultaneously convening a graduate seminar on preaching and ethics, it represents an attempt to reflect how ethics may be communicated in a sermon.

The opening story, which could be familiar to many, seeks to draw the reader dramatically into the critical edge of ethical behaviour and highlights the crucial role of *character*. Then the move to the biblical story in Luke 18 raises the systemic dimension of injustice to a higher level. One aspect of legal injustice is what it does to victims. This is illustrated in the case of Amina Lawal. This Nigerian woman lived for years under the threat of being stoned because of what appears to have been a false accusation. This helps the reader identify with the threat felt by the widow in Jesus' parable.

Christian ethics is inseparably connected to theology (*faith*), and this is introduced early in the sermon. Then the parable itself is engaged since scripture is the primary *authority* appealed to in this sermon. The analysis (*situation and context*) of the parable and of what lies behind gives a larger picture of how injustice might operate. This analysis also clarifies how God's covenant *norms* for justice and how appeals to God (*faith*) are empowering.

The implicit theology is now exposed on the larger canvas of history as a conflict between God and the principalities and powers. Resistance to these powers, as Charles Campbell and others have indicated, is a primary calling of the church. What this parable does is help expose the powers and, through the importunate widow, call attention to the spiritual nature of her resistance.

Ultimately, this is not about the widow as an example of fierce piety (that would lead in the direction of moralism) but about the storyteller who embodies his own preaching, especially in the cross and resurrection where the powers are finally subverted. The juxtaposition of what is happening in the world of the parable (and in our contemporary world) is set alongside the larger reality of the coming kingdom of God. This reflects James Kay's notion (in chapter 7) of a bifocal vision grounded in the cross.

So the sermon ends with a final appeal to our *experience* of feeling overwhelmed by the powers. The story from Central America demonstrates how one person of faith resisted the powers. The implication is clear: the coming Kingdom is glimpsed; the gospel finally enables justice.

In this process of this sermon all of the elements of ethical reflection explored in the preceding chapters are utilized—some more prominently than others. In the end Jesus, the preacher, is the heart and center of our ethical web, the one who enables us to proclaim and respond as faithful believers.

NOTES

Preface

[1] Terrance R. Anderson, *Walking the Way: Christian Ethics as a Guide* (Toronto: The United Church Publishing House, 1993).

Chapter 1: Preaching Ethics

[1] Bill Schiller, "Clone of Contention," *The Toronto Star,* 1 March 1997.

[2] Tanya Talaga and Lester Papp, "Genome Roadmap Will Take Science in New Directions," *The Toronto Star,* 26 June 2000; and Revelation 20:12.

[3] Jeremy Rifkin, "Cloning: Human Life as Patented Invention," *The Toronto Star,* 8 February 2000.

[4] Ibid. In an earlier piece, Rifkin comments, "The biotech revolution will force each of us to put a mirror to our most deeply held values, making us ponder the ultimate question of the meaning of existence" ("Cloned Genesis," *Maclean's Magazine* [May 4, 1998]: 52).

[5] Cf., Eileen L. Daniel, ed., *Taking Sides: Clashing Views on Controversial Issues in Health and Society,* 2d ed. (Guilford, Conn.: Dushkin/Brown & Benchmark, 1996).

[6] Joan Didion has raised serious concern over the lack of public debate in the period following this horrendous event of 9/11. See "Fixed Options, or the Hinge of History," *The New York Review of Books* (January 16, 2003): 54–59.

[7] See John Cassidy, "The Greed Cycle: How the Financial System Encouraged Corporations to Go Crazy," *The New Yorker* (September 23, 2002): 64–77.

[8] Alasdair MacIntyre, *After Virtue: A Study in Moral Theory,* 2d ed. (Notre Dame, Ind.: University of Notre Dame Press, 1984), 5. MacIntyre sights three examples: just war, abortion, and the justice of equal opportunity. On each of these he demonstrates unbridgeable impasses and internal confusion (p. 8).

[9] E.g., Thomas W. Ogletree, *The Use of the Bible in Christian Ethics* (Philadelphia: Fortress Press, 1983); and J. Philip Wogaman, *Speaking the Truth in Love: Prophetic Preaching to a Broken World* (Louisville, Ky.: Westminster John Knox Press, 1998).

[10] Cf., M. Douglas Meeks, *God the Economist: The Doctrine of God and Political Economy* (Minneapolis: Fortress Press), 78–80.

[11] On the significance of genre diversity in the Bible, see Paul Ricoeur, "Toward a hermeneutic of the idea of revelation," in *Essays on Biblical Interpretation,* ed. Lews S. Mudge (Philadelphia: Fortress Press, 1980), 73–118; Thomas Long, *Preaching and the Literary Forms of the Bible* (Philadelphia: Fortress Press, 1989); Don M. Wardlaw, ed., *Preaching Biblically: Creating Sermons in the Shape of Scripture* (Philadelphia: Westminster Press, 1983); and Richard Hays, *The Moral Vision of the New Testament: Community, Cross and New Creation; A Contemporary Introduction to New Testament Ethics* (San Francisco: Harper Collins, 1996).

[12] See J. Philip Wogaman, *Christian Ethics: A Historical Introduction* (Louisville, Ky.: Westminster John Knox Press, 1993), 2–15, for an extended treatment of these and other tensions.

[13] On the task of synthesizing the New Testament witness, see Richard B. Hays, *The Moral Vision of the New Testament* (New York: HarperCollins, 1996), 187–305.

[14] Wogaman, *Christian Ethics,* 270–76.

[15] Wogaman, *Christian Ethics.* I have used this work mostly without specific referencing to page numbers. His table of contents and index provide easy access for locating the relevant discussion.

[16] Cited by Wogaman, *Christian Ethics,* 37.

[17] See my treatment of Charles A. Cochrane's *Christianity and Classical Culture* in "Dilemmas of Preaching Doctrine: Declericalizing Proclamation," *Journal for Preachers* 17, no. 3 (Easter 1994): 31–32, 38.

[18] For David Hume, a secular ethic rooted solely in human need and human belief is just as adequate a basis for conduct as appeals to God. We do not need to know anything about the ultimate purpose of life to act morally. He sees spiritual need as a purely human phenomenon, while for Augustine it is kindled by grace. Now the modern study of religion becomes a purely human institution. See Michael Ignatieff, *The Needs of Strangers: An Essay on Privacy, Solidarity, and the Politics of Being Human* (New York: Penguin Books, 1984), 93, 97–98. Cf., MacIntyre, *After Virtue*, 226–37.

[19] Cf., David Heim's interview with Stanley Hauerwas, Robin Lovin, and Emilie Townes, "Ethics in Our Time: A Conversation on Christian Social Ethics," *The Christian Century* (September 27–October 4, 2000): 952–58.

[20] Cf., Martin E. Marty, "Clergy Ethics in America: The Ministers on Their Own," in *Clergy Ethics in a Changing Society: Mapping the Terrain*, ed. James P. Wind et al. (Louisville, Ky.: Westminster/John Knox Press, 1991), 27; and Peter L. Berger, "Secularization and the Problem of Plausibility," in *The Sacred Canopy* (Garden City, N.Y.: Doubleday, 1969), 127–53.

[21] As reported by Michael McAteer, "Separating Ethics from Religion," *The Toronto Star*, 25 November 2000. Buckman does, however, acknowledge that "humankind could not possibly have achieved such momentous advances in civilization in its comparatively short history were it not for the 'shorthand' of religious codes and behavior." He has written *Can We Be Good Without God?* (Toronto: Viking Press, 2000).

[22] MacIntyre, *After Virtue*, 243. This discussion follows his examination of Kierkegaard's view that "in the ethical life the commitments and responsibilities to the future" spring from past episodes uniting "the present to past and future in such a way as to make of a human life a unity" (p. 242).

[23] David Buttrick, *Homiletic: Moves and Structures* (Philadelphia: Fortress Press, 1987), 11–13.

[24] On the difference between faith and certitude, see Robert Towler, *The Need for Certainty: A Sociological Study of Conventional Religion* (London: Routledge & Kegan Paul, 1984).

[25] Elie Wiesel, *Night* (Toronto: Bantam Books, 1960, 1982), 62. Wiesel adds the narrator's inner response, "Where is He? Here He is—He is hanging here on this gallows..." But earlier in the novel the narrator says, "Some talked of God, of his mysterious ways, of the sins of the Jewish people, and of their future deliverance. But I had ceased to pray. How I sympathized with Job! I did not deny God's existence, but I doubted His absolute justice" (p. 42).

[26] Wayne G. Boulton, Thomas D. Kennedy, and Allen Verhey, eds., "An Introduction to Christian Ethics," in *From Christ to the World: Introductory Reading in Christian Ethics* (Grand Rapids, Mich.: Eerdmans, 1994), 1–3.

[27] Ibid., 4. The editors identify "the primary questions of ethics as 'Who am I as a follower of Jesus? What life is worthy of the one who recognizes the authority of Jesus? What sort of people should those who confess Jesus Christ be?'" (p. 5). Cf., Victor Paul Furnish, "Can Ethics Be Christian?" *The Christian Century* (October 26, 1994): 989–93.

[28] Reinhold Niebuhr, *An Interpretation of Christian Ethics* (New York: Living Age Books, 1956), 13–39. The inadequate responses that Niebuhr critiques throughout this book are "orthodox" (i.e., conservative) and "liberal" forms of Christianity. His alternative is prophetic faith. There is, of course, a larger question of what Christians can learn from other faith traditions. See, for example, Daniel Maguire, *The Moral Choice* (Minneapolis: Winston Press, 1979); and David Lochhead, *The Dialogical Imperative: A Christian Reflection on Interfaith Encounter* (Maryknoll, N.Y.: Orbis Books, 1988).

[29] Niebuhr, *An Interpretation of Christian Ethics*, 15.

[30] In the Introduction, I noted my indebtedness to a colleague, Terry Anderson, who calls this a "relational-responsibility method." See Anderson, *Walking the Way: Christian Ethics as a Guide* (Toronto: United Church Publishing House, 1993), 247–58. He argues that the five "base points" (as he calls them) "correspond to different facets of the actual moral life of persons" (p. 248). I have modified his approach (in order, language, imagery, etc.), but it remains essentially similar.

[31]Cf., Anderson, *Walking the Way*, 244–47; and Charles Campbell, *The Word Before the Powers: An Ethic of Preaching* (Louisville, Ky.: Westminster John Knox Press, 2002), who outlines three components for ethical preaching: recognizing the principalities and powers as spiritual forces in our world, resisting them, and recovering communities of resistance. I will take up these issues in later chapters.

[32]Cf., Arthur Van Seters, "Ethics," in *Concise Encyclopedia of Preaching*, ed. William H. Willimon and Richard Lischer (Louisville, Ky.: Westminster John Knox Press, 1995), 117–19, and my summary, "Grounded in *authoritative sources, basic convictions* shape *moral character* and *moral norms and standards* within a given *situation* set in a larger *social/cultural context.*"

[33]Barbara Brown Taylor, *The Luminous Web: Essays on Science and Religion* (Boston: Cowley, 2000), 60–62, 97. On interconnectedness, see further Rebecca Chopp, *Saving Work: Feminist Practices of Theological Education* (Louisville, Ky.: Westminster John Knox Press, 1995), 67–69.

[34]W. Walter Johnson, "The Ethics of Preaching," *Interpretation* 20 (1966): 416–17.

[35]Campbell, *Word before the Powers*, 44–67.

[36]Editorial, "A Vocation to Save Life," *The Christian Century* (March 24, 2000): 5. Note the similarity between this story and that of Ken Kim. The same kind of material can often illustrate different aspects of ethics. These overlaps are part of the intricate interconnectedness that the web image conveys.

[37]Anderson, *Walking the Way*, 226. Some ethicists see the interrelationship between these authorities as one of mutual correction. Cf., Lisa Sowle Cahill, "Moral Methodology: A Case Study," in *Introduction to Christian Ethics*, ed. Ronald P. Hamel and Kenneth R. Hines (Mahwah, N.J.: Paulist Press, 1989), 562.

[38]For a survey of these developments, see Don M. Wardlaw, "Homiletics and Preaching in North America," and Thomas G. Long, "Form," in *Concise Encyclopedia of Preaching*, 243–52 and 144–51, respectively.

[39]Here, I am echoing Campbell's perspective on preaching and will discuss the principalities and powers further, especially in chapter 5.

[40]Walter Brueggemann, "The Social Nature of the Biblical Text for Preaching," in *Preaching as a Social Act: Theology and Practice*, ed. Arthur Van Seters (Nashville: Abingdon Press, 1988), 138.

[41]Stanley Hauerwas, "The Ministry of a Congregation: Re-thinking Christian Ethics for a Church-Centered Seminary," in *Beyond Clericalism: The Congregation as a Focus for Theological Education*, ed. Joseph C. Hough Jr. and Barbara G. Wheeler (Chico, Calif.: Scholars Press, 1988), 123–34. Cf., Beverly W. Harrison, "Toward a Christian Feminist Liberation Hermeneutic for Demystifying Class Reality in Local Congregations," in *Beyond Clericalism*, 143.

Chapter 2: Faith

[1]Cf., William H. Willimon, *Peculiar Speech: Preaching to the Baptized* (Grand Rapids, Mich.: Eerdmans, 1992), 5–7, and Stephen Holmgren's comment that to "put on Christ," as symbolized in baptism, brings with it a new orientation and therefore a new behavior, *Ethics After Easter* (Boston: Cowley, 2000), 10–11.

[2]Preaching that creates a Christian worldview will be discussed again in chapter 5 when we deal with the worldviews of our culture. Some preachers may question whether we can assume that congregations view the world in a distinctively Christian way. Such an assumption may not be immediately obvious to others. When that is the case, sermons may have to take this reality seriously. But the contention here is that, in the final analysis, preaching *Christian* ethics assumes a commitment to Christian faith.

[3]Miroslav Volf, *Exclusion and Embrace: A Theological Exploration of Identity, Otherness, and Reconciliation* (Nashville: Abingdon Press, 1996), 9, cf. also 23.

[4]See numerous references in J. Philip Wogaman, *Christian Ethics: A Historical Introduction* (Louisville, Ky.: Westminster John Knox Press, 1993); Stanley Hauerwas, *The Peaceable Kingdom: A Primer in Christian Ethics* (Notre Dame, Ind.: University of Notre Dame Press, 1983), especially the final chapter; and Thomas Kennedy, "Can

War Be Just?" *From Christ to the World: Introductory Reading in Christian Ethics,* ed. Wayne G. Boulton, Thomas D. Kennedy, and Allen Verhey (Grand Rapids, Mich.: Eerdmans, 1994), 436–442. Here, preachers are often able to receive help from denominational or ecumenical documents that emerge in times of crisis.

[5] Mark A. Noll, *The Scandal of the Evangelical Mind* (Grand Rapids, Mich.: Eerdmans, 1994), 7. On theology in the modern/postmodern world, see *The Future of Theology: Essays in Honor of Jürgen Moltmann,* ed. Miroslav Volf, Carmen Krieg, and Thomas Kucharz (Grand Rapids, Mich.: Eerdmans, 1996), specifically the introduction by Volf; and Michael Welker, "Christian Theology: What Direction at the End of the Second Millennium?" esp. 73–76.

[6] I drew this case from Terry Anderson, *Walking the Way: Christian Ethics as a Guide* (Toronto: United Church Publishing House, 1993), 14–15.

[7] Cf., Daniel Patte, *Preaching Paul* (Philadelphia: Fortress Press, 1984), 13.

[8] Lewis S. Mudge, *The Church as Moral Community: Ecclesiology and Ethics in Ecumenical Debate* (New York: Continuum, 1998), 8–9, 32–33.

[9] Miroslav Volf, "Theology, Meaning, and Power," in *The Future of Theology,* 111.

[10] Jürgen Moltmann, "Theology and the Future of the Modern World," plenary address, American Academy of Religion/Society of Biblical Literature, November 21, 1994 (Pittsburgh: Association of Theological Schools), 1.

[11] To capture the sharpness of this alternative vision, see Charles Campbell, *The Word Before the Powers: An Ethic of Preaching* (Louisville, Ky.: Westminster John Knox Press, 2002), 48–51; and William R. Herzog II, *Parables as Subversive Speech: Jesus as Pedagogue of the Oppressed* (Louisville, Ky.: Westminster John Knox Press, 1994).

[12] Moltmann, "Theology and the Future of the Modern World," 5–6. Cf., Moltmann, *Theology of Hope,* trans. James W. Leitch (New York: Harper & Row, 1967); A. J. Conyers, *God, Hope, and History* (Macon, Ga.: Mercer University Press, 1988); Ingolf U. Dalferth, "Time for God's Presence," in *The Future of Theology,* 140.

[13] Jack Lakey, "Do Kids Gamble? Do You Wanna Bet?" *The Toronto Star,* 6 October 2001.

[14] Walter Stefaniuk, "Gambling Take: $5.47 Billion," *The Toronto Star,* 17 January 2003, (for the fiscal year 2001–2002).

[15] *The Globe and Mail,* 27 March 2000, and *The Toronto Star,* 19 February, 9 March, 19 April, 10 July, and 14 October 2000. The first Ontario lottery began in 1975 with net revenues that year of $43 million.

[16] "The Cost of Gambling," *Health Magazine* (April 1998): 16. This news report quotes Phillips, "For large numbers of people, gambling is a pleasure they can take or leave. For a small number, it is an addiction that causes tremendous pain." This kind of comment is strange when put alongside of many other statistics, not only on suicide but also on bankruptcies, broken homes, serious depression, etc. Recently I heard that the annual social cost of gambling in the state of California is $5 billion.

[17] Cf., John Cassidy, "The Greed Cycle," *The New Yorker* (September 23, 2002): 64–77. Other rationalizations include the need to pay down massive debts, but such arguments have been exposed as fabrications by studies such as Linda McQuaig's *Shooting the Hippo: Death by Deficit and Other Canadian Myths* (Toronto: Penguin Books, 1995). Government assistance to social and cultural projects is increasingly funded from this revenue, and some denominations regard this as discrimination against those who oppose gambling of whatever kind.

[18] Editorial, "Fortuna's Rule," *The Christian Century* (November 11, 1998): 1045–46.

[19] Phyllis Vineberg, "My Son Could Not Resist Gambling's Siren Song," *The Toronto Star,* 26 May 2000.

[20] As noted in chapter 1, Alasdair MacIntyre states that a sense of purpose was once an integral aspect of a sacral view of life. It saw the lives of human beings related to the life of God. When secular ethics weakened this relationship and finally dissolved it over a period of three centuries, the link between ethics and theology broke. At that point ethics became expendable. See Alasdair MacIntyre, *After Virtue: A Study in Moral Theory,* 2d ed. (Notre Dame, Ind.: University of Notre Dame Press, 1984), 60–61.

²¹Cf., Douglas John Hall, "Christian Mission in a Post-Christendom World," *The Ecumenist* 38, no. 2 (Spring 2001): 1–4.

²²See Ted Peters, "Concupiscence: Lusting for What They Have," chapter 5 in *Sin: Radical Evil in Soul and Society* (Grand Rapids, Mich.: Eerdmans, 1994). Obviously, this chapter would also be helpful for business people wanting to transcend the greed factor in economic transactions.

²³James Luther Mays, *Psalms: Interpretation, A Bible Commentary for Teaching and Preaching* (Louisville, Ky.: John Knox Press, 1994), 65–70.

²⁴Jürgen Moltmann, *God in Creation: A New Theology of Creation and the Spirit of God* (San Francisco: Harper & Row, 1985), 234–43; Stanley J. Grenz, *Theology for the Community of God* (Nashville: Broadman & Holman, 1994), 100–102, 125–27, 218–34; and Arthur Van Seters, "The Doctrine of the Trinity: The Basis for Christian Stewardship," (a booklet published in Toronto by the Presbyterian Church in Canada, 1999).

²⁵Anderson, *Walking the Way,* 164–65.

²⁶Herbert Ehnes, "The Alliance Since 1970," *Reformed World* 49 (1999): 137–38.

²⁷Margaret Somerville, *The Ethical Canary: Science, Society and the Human Spirit* (Toronto: Viking, 2000), 18–21.

²⁸Canadian Council of Churches, *Life Patent Pending: A Discussion Guide on Biotechnology and the Oncomouse* (Toronto: Canadian Council of Churches, n.d.). The name Oncomouse refers to oncology because the gene sequence of the mouse was modified so that its offspring would be susceptible to cancer. Some would argue that creating possibility for suffering in animals even for a good cause is ethically unacceptable.

²⁹Richard Crossman, "Thinking about Bioethics: A Way Forward," in *Life Patent Pending,* 14–16.

³⁰"Human Cloning and Biotechnology," in *The Acts and Proceedings of the 126th General Assembly of the Presbyterian Church in Canada* (Toronto: The Presbyterian Church in Canada, 2000), 333–34. Cf., Somerville, *The Ethical Canary,* chap. 3, and John Habgood, *Being a Person: Where Faith and Science Meet* (London: Hodder & Stoughton, 1998), chap. 12. We focus here on human nature, but genetic studies affecting animal and plant life are also important.

³¹As with many other moral questions, a major factor in the genomic debate over ethics is the enormous prospect for financial gain on the part of biotechnology pharmaceutical companies. When Former President Bill Clinton and Prime Minister Tony Blair expressed the view that the genome should not be private property, stocks in companies such as the Celera Genomics Group tumbled. Cf., Richard Preston, "The Genome Warrior," *The New Yorker* (June 12, 2000): 67–76; and Stuart Laidlaw, "Prospecting for Genetic Gold," *The Toronto Star,* 14 December 2000.

³²The scientific developments and debates surrounding therapeutic cloning continue at a rapid pace. Ethical questions have become an integral aspect of these explorations. See, for example, Jose B. Cibelli, Robert P. Lanza, Michael West, with Carol Ezzell, "The First Human Cloned Embryo," *Scientific American* (January 2002)–downloaded from the Internet, www.sciamdigital.com.

³³Cf., Walter Brueggemann, *Israel's Praise, Doxology Against Idolatry and Ideology* (Philadelphia: Fortress Press, 1988), 6–11.

³⁴Campbell, *Word Before the Powers,* 24–43.

³⁵I am indebted to Terry Anderson for his analysis of these matters in *Walking the Way,* 173–86.

³⁶It is also possible that the democratic process may foster a blindness to social sin. See the discussion of ideology in chapter 5.

³⁷See John Cassidy, "The Greed Cycle: How the Financial System Encouraged Corporations to Go Crazy," *The New Yorker* (September 23, 2002): 64–77. See also Barbara Ley Toffler with Jennifer Reingold, *Final Accounting: Ambition, Greed, and the Fall of Arthur Andersen* (New York: Broadway Books, 2003).

³⁸See the example of Michelle Brill-Edwards in chapter 3, p. 57.

[39]Philip Wogaman, *Speaking the Truth in Love: Prophetic Preaching to a Broken World* (Louisville, Ky.: Westminster John Knox Press, 1998), 143–52.

[40]See Wogaman's sermon, "The Vocation of Politics," in *Speaking the Truth in Love*, 175–83.

[41]John S. McClure and Nancy J. Ramsay, eds., *Telling the Truth: Preaching about Sexual and Domestic Violence* (Cleveland: United Church Press, 1998).

[42]Nancy Ramsay, "Sexual Abuse and Shame: The Travail of Recovery," in *Women in Travail and Transition: A New Pastoral Care*, ed. Maxine Glaz and Jeanne Stevenson Moessner (Minneapolis: Fortress Press, 1991).

[43]Marie Fortune, "Preaching Forgiveness?" *Telling the Truth*, 49.

[44]Wendy Farley, "Evil, Violence and the Practice of Theodicy," in *Telling the Truth*, 12–14.

[45]Ibid., 15–19.

[46]Fortune, "Preaching Forgiveness?" 54–55.

[47]John S. McClure, "Preaching about Sexual and Domestic Violence," in *Telling the Truth*, 115.

[48]Being judgmental is different from identifying with God's hatred of sin. The former arises out of a sense of superiority, the latter out of an awareness of God's holiness. The congregation needs the latter.

Chapter 3: Moral Character

[1]See Charles Campbell's deeply moving account of how a congregation in Le Chambon sur Lignon, France, resisted the Nazi powers in saving the lives of five thousand Jews in World War II. They could do this because of the kind of moral formation that had shaped the congregation's life. *The Word Before the Powers: An Ethic of Preaching* (Louisville, Ky.: Westminster John Knox Press, 2002), 1–2.

[2]Stephen Carter, *Integrity* (New York: Basic Books, 1996), ix–x.

[3]Ibid., ix.

[4]Ibid., 4–5, 7.

[5]Christie Blatchford, "A Courtroom's Gretzky," *The National Post*, 5 May 2000.

[6]Alan Young, "The Lessons from the Murray Case," *The Toronto Star*, 14 June 2000.

[7]This case illustrates the area of normative obligations to which we will turn in the next chapter. We use it here to point to the prerequisite of moral character that enables us to fulfill our obligations.

[8]Edward Pellegrino, "The Place of Virtue in Medical Ethics: The Ethics of the Professions, Especially Medicine," a taped public lecture delivered at St. Marks College, University of British Columbia, in the early 1990s. The following summarizes Pellegrino's argument based on a tape of his presentation.

[9]Did both Ken Murray and Austin Cooper lose sight of the *telos* of the legal profession? Did they both fail to discharge their stewardship to use knowledge for the purpose of justice? Did they just try to win at all costs? The presiding judge spelled out the court's decision that lawyers cannot place the interests of their clients above the right to a fair trial for all who come before the courts. See, Editorial, "Lesson for Lawyers," *The Toronto Star*, 15 June 2000.

[10]Pellegrino used *patient* rather than *client* because, he argued, the latter has the root meaning of being an economic vassal. This economic connotation also affects other professions such as law.

[11]Pellegrino listed the kind of virtues that rightly can be expected of physicians: *benevolence* (thinking of the person to be healed), *fidelity to trust* (deeper than written contracts), *effacement of self-interest* (so as not to take advantage of the vulnerability of the patient), *compassion* (the capacity to feel something of the pain and suffering of another person), and *prudence* (the capacity to make a right decision in a complex situation).

¹²Terry Anderson, *Walking the Way: Christian Ethics as a Guide* (Toronto: United Church Publishing House, 1993), 143. In a discussion following his lecture, Pellegrino acknowledged that Christians move beyond ancient Greek notions of virtue to one that accepts a view of human nature in which we are both natural and supernatural beings. Christians also discern the virtue of charity, which is a deeper love than benevolence, one that emerges from a commitment to faith in Christ.

¹³For the following analysis of the distinctively Christian nature of moral character, I am indebted to Stanley Hauerwas, *The Peaceable Kingdom: A Primer in Christian Ethics* (Notre Dame, Ind.: University of Notre Dame Press, 1983), especially chapters 1-3.

¹⁴Cf., Miroslav Volf, "The Self and Its Center," in *Exclusion and Embrace: A Theological Exploration of Identity, Otherness, and Reconciliation* (Nashville: Abingdon Press, 1996), 69-71.

¹⁵This can also be seen in a wonderful conversation about seeing reality whole as God sees it, presented by Chaim Potok in his novel *The Gift of Asher Lev* (New York: Fawcett Crest, 1990), 97-98. Potok's novels reveal the Hasidic community as an extension of the Jewish family, one profoundly formative in molding the character of devout Jews.

¹⁶Hauerwas, *Peaceable Kingdom*, 45. On this point Hauerwas is closer to Alasdair MacIntyre than Pellegrino. For the latter, virtue is the responsibility of the individual professional person (though within a professional association), while the former believes that personal virtue requires a supportive community (*After Virtue: A Study in Moral Theory*, 2d ed. [Notre Dame, Ind.: University of Notre Dame Press, 1984], 63).

¹⁷Reinhold Niebuhr, *The Nature and Destiny of Man*, vol. 1 (New York: Charles Scribner's Sons, 1964), 178-79.

¹⁸Barbara Ley Toffler with Jennifer Reingold, *Final Accounting: Ambition, Greed, and the Fall of Arthur Andersen* (New York: Broadway Books, 2003). For a similar disclosure of character *de-formation* see the television production of "The Crooked E: The Unshredded Truth about Enron," CTV, January 5, 2003.

¹⁹William H. Willimon, "Why Don't They Know Him?" a sermon preached at Yorkminster Park Baptist Church, October 15, 2000, and available on tape.

²⁰See especially James L. Mays, *The Lord Reigns: A Theological Handbook to the Psalms* (Louisville: Westminster John Knox Press, 1994), chap. 2, "The Center of the Psalms: 'The Lord Reigns' as Root Metaphor," 12-22.

²¹Anderson, *Walking the Way*, 116-17.

²²This is especially evident in "Freedom," the final section of Mandela's *Long Walk to Freedom* (New York: Little, Brown, 1994).

²³Anderson, *Walking the Way*, 117-18.

²⁴See also conventional lists of vices: Mk. 7:21-22; Rom. 1:29-31; 1 Cor. 6:9-10; and 2 Cor. 12:20; and of virtues: Rom. 12:6-8; 1 Cor. 12:7-11; and 2 Pet. 1:5-8.

²⁵Charles B. Cousar, *Galatians: Interpretation, A Bible Commentary for Teaching and Preaching* (Atlanta: John Knox Press, 1992), 137-38.

²⁶Hauerwas, *Peaceable Kingdom*, 102-6, draws particular attention to the four cardinal virtues of prudence, justice, self-control, and courage. He points also to the eschatological virtues of gratitude-humility, hope, vigilance, and serenity and joy. Cf., Anderson, *Walking the Way*, 117-37.

²⁷Alyce M. McKenzie, "Out of Character! Preaching Biblical Wisdom in a Secular Age," *Journal for Preachers* 22, no. 4 (Pentecost 1999): 44-50. In a subsequent article, "The Character of the Preacher," *Journal for Preachers* 24, no. 3 (Pentecost 2001): 19-30, McKenzie notes four aspects of wisdom: God is its source; we have human limitations in discernment; diverse perspectives are important; and we need a listening, seeking heart.

²⁸Alyce M. McKenzie, *Preaching Proverbs: Wisdom for the Pulpit* (Louisville: Westminster John Knox, 1996), part three.

²⁹Cf., Walter Wink's analysis of "the myth of redemptive violence in popular culture today" in *Engaging the Powers: Discernment and Resistance in a World of Domination*

(Minneapolis: Fortress Press, 1992), 17–25; Anthony Lewis, "Bush and Iraq," *The New York Review of Books,* 7 November 2002, 6; and John Cassidy, "The Greed Cycle: How the Financial System Encouraged Corporations to Go Crazy," *The New Yorker* (September 23, 2002): 64–77.

[30] E.g., J. Alfred Smith, "Good news for bad times," *The Overflowing Heart: Gospel Messages that Encourage the Abundant Life* (Nashville: Broadman Press, 1987), pp. 61–64.

[31] B. A. Gerrish, "Sin," in *The Pilgrim Road: Sermons of Christian Life* (Louisville, Ky.: Westminster John Knox Press, 2000), 85–91.

[32] Rebecca Bragg, "Ex-Bureaucrat Turns Public Warrior," *The Toronto Star,* 30 January 1997.

[33] See further Richard Lischer, "The Sermon on the Mount as Radical Pastoral Care," *Interpretation* 41, no. 2 (April 1987): 160–63; he insists that to avoid a moralistic interpretation of the Sermon on the Mount, we must read it within an eschatological understanding of the church as called and enabled by Christ to live for the kingdom that he has inaugurated and will complete.

[34] Cousar, *Galatians,* 134–35.

[35] Ted Peters, *Sin: Radical Evil in Soul and Society* (Grand Rapids, Mich.: Eerdmans, 1994), 1–4. Peters wrote this in response to the increasing popularity of New Age self-help books and programs that fail to take sin seriously and hence have no room for a doctrine of redemption. He was also confronting the growing phenomenon of Satanism.

[36] Gracia Grindal, "Preaching the Word in Good and True Words," *Word and World* 10, no. 3 (Summer 1990): 237–45.

Chapter 4: Norms

[1] Bill Evans, "Improvisation in Jazz," liner notes on the original 1959 LP of Miles Davis, *A Kind of Blue,* reproduced as a CD disc (New York: Columbia Recording, 1997).

[2] Will D. Campbell, *Brother to a Dragonfly* (New York: Continuum, 1997), 225–27. How Campbell came to this discovery is itself a moving vignette (pp. 214–28). But the law, as Calvin understood it, can also be viewed as a gift of grace. See note 12.

[3] On definitions see Terry Anderson, *Walking the Way: Christian Ethics as a Guide* (Toronto: United Church Publishing House, 1993), 283–87.

[4] For preaching on the stewardship of creation, see Dieter T. Hessel, ed., *For Creation's Sake: Preaching, Ecology, & Justice* (Philadelphia: Geneva Press, 1985).

[5] Leonard J. Brooks, "Forget Compliance, Think Governance," *The Corporate Ethics Monitor* (July–August 2002): 1. On the weakening of the Securities and Exchange Commission in the U.S., Jane Mayer, "The Accountant's War," *The New Yorker* (April 22 and 29, 2002); and Jeffrey Toobin, "The Man Chasing Enron," 9 September 2002, 86–94. Lawmakers must also be held accountable given the unprecedented level of corporate influence on the election of politicians across North America—see David Olive, "Last Rights for the New Economy," *The Toronto Star,* 24–27 August 2002.

[6] Cf., Reinhold Niebuhr, *An Interpretation of Christian Ethics* (New York: Living Age Books, 1956), 98–99.

[7] On the transformative implications of a biblical doctrine of grace to clarify the "law of Christ," see Ellen Charry, "The Grace of God and the Law of Christ," *Interpretation* 57, no. 1 (January 2003): 34–44.

[8] Stanley Hauerwas points out that without this larger end or purpose, rules represent merely an agreement of what is essential to ensure society's harmony and survival. This has given rise to two ways of formulating rules: 1. *Duty, what we ought to do because we ought to do it* (deontology). We do what we promise to do simply because we promised to do it (apart from aims or intentions); this is our duty. 2. *Use, the consequences of our actions determine how we act* (utilitarianism or consequentialism). Moral rules are but generalizations of our experience of what produces the greatest happiness for the greatest number. We keep promises because that produces better results. See *The Peaceable Kingdom: A Primer in Christian Ethics* (Notre Dame, Ind.: University of

Notre Dame Press, 1983), 20–21. A third option, *proportionalism,* combines actions, intentions, and consequences. Cf., Anderson, *Walking the Way,* 246.

[9]Niebuhr, *Interpretation of Christian Ethics,* 99, 112.

[10]To borrow a phrase from Tom Chappell, *The Soul of a Business: Managing for Profit and for the Common Good* (New York: Bantam Books, 1993), 18.

[11]Cf., J. Clinton McCann Jr., "The Hermeneutics of Grace: Discerning the Bible's Single Plot," *Interpretation* 37, no. 1 (January 2003): esp. 5–9; Walter Brueggemann, "Duty as Delight and Desire (Preaching Obedience That Is Not Legalism)," *Journal for Preachers* 18, no. 1 (1994): 1–14, on the covenantal context of the Ten Commandments and its implications for preaching.

[12]John Calvin, *Institutes of the Christian Religion,* vol. 1, trans. Henry Beverage (Grand Rapids, Mich.: Eerdmans, 1957), 304–13. For an especially poignant example of the first use of the law, see William J. Carl III, "The Decalogue in Liturgy, Preaching and Life," *Interpretation* 58, no. 3 (July 1989): 274–78.

[13]Cf., Patricia Dutcher-Walls, *The Commandments for a Blessed Life: A Resource Book* (Pittsburgh: Kerygma Program, 1999).

[14]Walter Brueggemann, *Theology of the Old Testament: Testimony, Dispute, Advocacy* (Minneapolis: Fortress Press, 1997), 581–90. Brueggemann designates the command tradition as ethical and the instruction tradition as aesthetic and artistic. A central part of my argument is that ethics should be understood more broadly. Aesthetic and artistic forms may also enable ethical formation and celebration as Brueggemann himself demonstrates in his comments on the Ten Commandments in *Finally Comes the Poet: Daring Speech for Proclamation* (Minneapolis: Fortress Press, 1989), 79–101, and *Interpretation and Obedience* (Minneapolis: Fortress Press, 1991), 145–58.

[15]Fleming Rutledge, "Rules of the Freedom Game," *The Bible and the New York Times* (Grand Rapids, Mich.: Eerdmans, 1998), 104–10. This is a homiletic illustration of the principle of jazz improvisation noted at the beginning of this chapter.

[16]At one time the Decalogue, or its summary in the two great commandments, was read in many churches as a regular part of the liturgy. These were reminders of our specific obligations as God's people.

[17]Richard Lischer, "The Sermon on the Mount as Radical Pastoral Care," *Interpretation* 41, no. 2 (April 1987): 158–63.

[18]See Lisa Sowle Cahill, "The Ethical Implications of the Sermon on the Mount," *Interpretation* 41, no. 2 (April 1987): 144–56. Cf., Charry, "Grace of God," 39–41.

[19]William H. Willimon, "Matthew 7:43–48," *Interpretation* 57, no. 1 (January 2003): 61–63. This is especially cogent when many in the world respond to their perceived enemies with fear, hate, and war.

[20]Ted Peters, *Sin: Radical Evil in Soul and Society* (Grand Rapids, Mich.: Eerdmans, 1994), 302–6.

[21]Brueggemann, "Duty as Delight and Desire," 3.

[22]For these and other references I am drawing on a series of articles in *The Toronto Star,* 17–25 January 2001.

[23]Arthur Schaffer, "The Top Judges Got It Wrong in This Case," *The Toronto Star,* 19 January 2001.

[24]From the perspective of situation and context (see chap. 5), we would be analyzing this extensively in terms of individualism, viewing people as property, media influence, secularity, and the loss of a sense of mystery, especially the mystery of death. Cf., Margaret Somerville, *The Ethical Canary: Science, Society and the Human Spirit* (Toronto: Viking, 2000), 120–29.

[25]This Bill Moyers program was aired September 11–13, 2000, and was reviewed with commentary by Keith G. Meador and L. Gregory Jones, "Bearing Witness in Life and Death," *The Christian Century,* 16–23 August 2000, 830–32. Cf., also two other *Christian Century* articles: Richard M. Gula, "Dying Well: A Challenge to Christian Compassion," (May 5, 1999): 501–5; and Allen Verhey, "Choosing Death: The Ethics of Assisted Suicide" (July 17, 1996): 716–19; as well as Gilbert Meilaender, "The Distinction Between Killing and Allowing to Die," in *From Christ to the World: Introductory*

Reading in Christian Ethics, ed. Wayne G. Boulton, Thomas D. Kennedy, and Allen Verhey (Grand Rapids, Mich.: Eerdmans, 1994), 404–6.

[26] Cf., Jean Vanier's 1998 CBC Massey Lectures, *Becoming Human* (Toronto: Anansi, 1998).

[27] On this witness in the early church, see Margaret Visser, *The Geometry of Love: Space, Time, Mystery, and Meaning in an Ordinary Church* (Toronto: Harper Flamingo Canada, 2000), 48–52, 215.

[28] See McCann's assertion that a failure to discern God's essential nature as merciful, gracious, and loving is what leads inevitably to a doctrine of retribution, "Hermeneutics of Grace," 15.

[29] Miroslav Volf, *Exclusion and Embrace: A Theological Exploration of Identity, Otherness, and Reconciliation* (Nashville: Abingdon Press, 1996), 216, 220. See also, Gordon Graham, "Justice and Christian Charity," in *From Christ to the World,* 260–63. Restorative justice does not mean that there is no punishment but that the purpose of punishment is restoration of both victim and accused, not retribution. See further the following discussion.

[30] Karen Lebacqz, "Implications for a Theory of Justice," in *From Christ to the World,* 254–55 (reprinted from her volume, *Justice in an Unjust World* [Minneapolis: Augsburg, 1987]). Lebacqz goes on to spell out an approach to justice that searches for the roots of justice and includes right relationship, covenant responsibilities, dealing with exploitation, the need for liberation, and always looking for another jubilee corrective (p. 257).

[31] Volf, *Exclusion and Embrace,* 221–22.

[32] Ibid., 220–25.

[33] Tonda MacCharles, "Supreme Court Raises Issue of Clemency in Emotional Case," *The Toronto Star,* 19 January 2001.

[34] See the wonderful conversation between a rabbi and an artist regarding the difference between human seeing and God's in Chaim Potok's novel, *The Gift of Asher Lev* (New York: Fawcett Crest, 1990), 97–98.

[35] Cf., Derek L. Phillips, *Toward a Just Social Order* (Princeton, N.J.: Princeton University Press, 1986), 37–41; and Alasdair MacIntyre, *After Virtue: A Study in Moral Theory,* 2d ed. (Notre Dame, Ind.: University of Notre Dame Press, 1984), 34–35.

[36] Stephen Carter, *Integrity* (New York: Basic Books, 1996), 60–61, 238.

[37] Anderson, *Walking the Way,* 76–85. These specifics may be regarded by some as too controversial for a sermon. See my approach to preaching on poverty and welfare in chapter 5.

[38] This positive development is sometimes linked to a voluntary approach to regulations. Companies such as Talisman Energy of Canada have learned how to present their values in a colorful CSR Report but hide their failure to comply with international standards on human rights abuses. See Kairos: Canadian Ecumenical Justice Initiatives, *Benchmarks: Corporate Responsibility, A Field Action Guide* (Toronto: Kairos-Canada), 18.

[39] All four of these have been given as justifications for deciding on values according to Phillips, *Toward a Just Social Order,* 11–28.

[40] Carol Goar, "Stop Giving Us Tax Breaks," *The Toronto Star,* 24 April 1999. The editorial says nothing about the religious commitment of this group, but their actions certainly point to gospel values. Cf., also John Peters, "Why Tax Cuts Just Don't Work," *The Toronto Star,* 20 January 2003.

[41] Chappell, *The Soul of a Business,* esp. 12–27. For more information on CSR, see Deb Abby, contributing ed., *Global Profit and Global Justice* (Gabriola Is., B.C.: New Society Publishers, 2004). For a broad discussion of theology and business, see two articles in *The Christian Century* (March 27 and April 2, 2002): Daniel Rush Finn, "God and Goods: Economics as If Theology Mattered," 24–28; and Stewart Herman, "Corporate Citizen: The Moral Life of a Stockholder," 29–31. An extraordinary review of recent publications on the larger question of how theology interacts with economics

is offered by Jeorg Rieger, "Theology and Economics," *Religious Studies Review* 28, no. 3 (July 2002): 215–20.

⁴²John B. Cobb Jr., *Sustaining the Common Good: A Christian Perspective on the Global Economy* (Cleveland: Pilgrim Press), 17–19. Cobb grounds this perspective not only in scripture but also in the panentheistic notion that "all that happens in the created order enters fully into the divine life" (p. 21).

⁴³Michael Ignatieff, *The Rights Revolution* (Toronto: House of Anansi Press, 2000), 92–93.

⁴⁴Anderson, *Walking the Way*, 91.

⁴⁵Lesslie Newbigin, *Foolishness to the Greeks: The Gospel and Western Culture* (London: SPCK, 1986), 118–22.

⁴⁶Paton's *Cry, the Beloved Country* (New York: Charles Scribner's Sons, 1948) focuses on black South Africans, and Kogawa's *Obasan* (Markham, Ont.: Penguin Books, 1983) and *Itsuka* (Toronto: Penguin Books, 1993) wrestle with the treatment of Japanese Canadians during and after World War II. Both authors write out of a clear, theological perspective.

⁴⁷William Sloane Coffin, *A Passion for the Possible: A Message to the U.S. Churches* (Louisville, Ky.: Westminster/John Knox Press, 1993), 85–88. He also asks, "Don't good shepherds have a certain duty to drive out the wolves to make room for more sheep?"

Chapter 5: Situation and Context

¹Dietrich Bonhoeffer, *Ethics,* trans. N. H. Smith (New York: MacMillan, 1955), 364–65, cited in the introduction: "The Contexts of Christian Ethics," of Wayne G. Boulton, Thomas D. Kennedy, and Allen Verhey, eds., *From Christ to the World: Introductory Reading in Christian Ethics* (Grand Rapids, Mich.: Eerdmans, 1994), 281.

²Ronald J. Sider, *Rich Christians in an Age of Hunger* (New York: Paulist Press, 1978).

³Charles Elliott, *Praying the Kingdom: Towards a Political Spirituality* (New York: Paulist Press, 1985), 8.

⁴This kind of birth used to be called Siamese twins–an ethnic designation I have avoided using.

⁵E.g., Isa. 53 and Jn. 11:50.

⁶Richard Lischer, in "The Limits of Story," reminds us that "stories may be the inspiration for change...but they are not equipped to make the kinds of discrimination necessary for informed ethical decisions": *Interpretation* 38, no. 1 (January 1984): 35.

⁷Liz Theoharis, "There Was No Poor Person among Them," *Church and Society* 91 (November/December 2000): 40.

⁸Kim Bobo, "Living Wages, Inside and Outside the Church," *Church and Society* 91 (November/December 2000): 49.

⁹The current U.S. administration's recent massive tax cuts have increased these disparities even further.

¹⁰For what follows, I am indebted particularly to Gregory Baum, "Three Theses on Contextual Theology," *The Ecumenist* 24, no. 1 (Spring 1986): 51–55; and to Terry Anderson, *Walking the Way: Christian Ethics as a Guide* (Toronto: United Church Publishing House, 1993), 195–205.

¹¹Derek Philips, *Toward a Just Social Order* (Princeton, N.J.: Princeton University Press, 1986), 341–78, discusses, among others, the views of Alan Gewirth, Robert Nozick, John Rawls, and Richard Della Fave.

¹²Rory Leishman, "A Time for Forgiveness and Reconciliation," *The London Free Press,* 10 April 2001. He adds, "A more reliable mark of generosity is the extent of one's disposition to donate some of his or her own after-tax income to charity. By this measure, some people who are quick to accuse conservatives of lacking in generosity and compassion for the poor might not appear quite so altruistic and tender-hearted themselves."

[13] J. Mark Thomas notes that Herbert Spencer once pointed out that this notion of merit is the central tenet of a theory of economic and social justice in a market system. He also cites John Hospers: "In a free-enterprise society...a person's financial success is determined...by his value to others...as they themselves estimate their value." See Thomas, "Myth and Mythos of Meritocracy," *The Ecumenist* 26, no. 1 (November-December 1987): 1.

[14] E.g., Thomas states that in San Francisco 85 percent of employers "hired *no* employees through the want ads in a typical year." He calls the so-called *free*-market for labor a myth. "Myth and Mythos of Meritocracy," 2.

[15] John Ralston Saul, "The Collapse of Globalism and the Rebirth of Nationalism," *Harper's* (March 2004): 34.

[16] H. Eberhard Von Waldow, "Social Responsibility and Social Structure in Early Israel," *Catholic Biblical Quarterly* 32, no. 2 (April 1970): 182–203.

[17] Many biblical narratives and proverbial passages correlate wealth, wisdom, and righteousness—though this is severely critiqued within the Bible, most notably in the book of Job.

[18] I am deliberately avoiding the language of self-sufficiency often used here because it reflects the cultural legacy of Enlightenment individualism.

[19] Carl Dudley, "The Welfare Revolution: Essential Conversions," *The Christian Century*, 15 October 1997, 900–902. Amy L. Sherman makes the comment, "If the church is to respond effectively to the new challenges faced by families on welfare, it must initiate targeted, holistic, relationally based programs that help the poor move toward a permanent transformation," in "Welfare to Work: A Report from the Front Lines," *The Christian Century*, 15 October 1997, 906. Cf., also Arthur E. Farnsley II, "Faith-Based Action: Different Groups Have Different Agendas"; Carl S. Dudley, "Charitable Choice: A Closer Look," *The Christian Century* (March 14, 2001): 12–18; and Heidi Rolland Unruh, "Choosing Partners: Church and State Working Together," *The Christian Century*, 4–17 December 2002, 8–9.

[20] Gordon Graham, "Justice and Christian Charity," in *From Christ to the World*, 260–63, excerpted from Graham's *The Idea of Christian Charity* (Notre Dame, Ind: Notre Dame Univ. Press, 1990). This argument challenges a rights approach to justice, which is more reflective of liberalism than a biblical view of grounding justice in the righteousness of God. But I also think that a case can be made for justice as care for the poor based on their needs within covenantal responsibilities.

[21] Otto Maduro notes that prophetic innovation arises when other movements in society are traveling in a certain direction. The prophet, then, provides a creative, alternative vision that inspires and energizes change. *Religion and Social Conflicts*, trans. Robert R. Barr (Maryknoll, N.Y.: Orbis Books), 106–9.

[22] David Baker, "Affordable Justice: A Modest Proposal," *The Toronto Star*, 16 February 2001.

[23] William Stringfellow, *An Ethic for Christians and Other Aliens in a Strange Land* (Waco, Tex.: Word Books, 1973), 69. Cf., Charles L. Campbell, "Principalities and Powers, and Preaching: Learning from William Stringfellow," *Interpretation* 51, no. 4 (October 1997): 384–401.

[24] Another aspect of worldview is postmodernism. For an analysis of postmodernist thinking, see J. Richard Middleton and Brian J. Walsh, *Truth Is Stranger Than It Used to Be: Biblical Faith in a Postmodern Age* (Downers Grove, Ill.: Inter-Varsity Press, 1995); and Stanley J. Grenz, *A Primer on Postmodernism* (Grand Rapids, Mich.: Eerdmans, 1996). Two homileticians that follow a postmodernist perspective are Ronald Allen, "Preaching and Postmodernism," *Interpretation* 55, no. 1 (January 2001): 35–48; and John S. McClure, *Other-wise Preaching: A Postmodern Ethic for Homiletics* (St. Louis: Chalice Press, 2001).

[25] Phyllis Trible, *God and the Rhetoric of Sexuality* (Philadelphia: Fortress Press, 1978).

[26] Rebecca S. Chopp, *Saving Work: Feminist Practices of Theological Education* (Louisville, Ky.: Westminster John Knox Press, 1995), 85.

²⁷Paulo Freire, *Pedagogy of Hope: Reliving Pedagogy of the Oppressed*, trans. Robert R. Barr (New York: Continuum, 1995), 102–5. Freire admits that after publishing his earlier work in the 1960s, he received many letters from feminist writers who drew his attention to sexist influences. He responds, "The rejection of a sexist ideology, which necessarily involves a re-creation of language, is part of the possible dream of a change of the world" (p. 67).

²⁸On gender and preaching, see Leonora Tubbs Tisdale, "Women's Ways of Communicating: A New Blessing for Preaching," in *Women, Gender, and Christian Community*, ed. Jane Dempsey Douglass and James F. Kay (Louisville, Ky.: Westminster John Knox Press, 1997), 104–16; on race, see Allan Boesak, "Introduction: Relevant Preaching in a Black Context," *The Finger of God: Sermons on Faith and Socio-Political Responsibility*, trans. Peter Randall (Maryknoll, N.Y.: Orbis Books, 1982), 1–17.

²⁹Walter Wink, *Engaging the Powers: Discernment and Resistance in a World of Domination* (Minneapolis: Fortress Press, 1992), 1–10. Wink names five worldviews: ancient, spiritualistic, materialistic, theological, and integral.

³⁰Jon Sobrino, "Awakening from the Sleep of Inhumanity," *The Christian Century*, (April 3, 1991): 364–66. I identify with Sobrino's story. When I was faced with poverty in Central America in 1981, I suddenly saw the pervasiveness of poverty in the Bible. It was like reading a book I had never read before.

³¹Stanley Hauerwas challenges our ability to communicate the gospel and be understood as a merely human exchange when, in fact, the gospel can only transform us through the activity we call conversion. See *Preaching to Strangers* (Louisville, Ky.: Westminster/John Knox Press, 1992), 10.

³²See Mark Noll's comments about cultural influence, *The Scandal of the Evangelical Mind* (Grand Rapids, Mich.: Eerdmans, 1994), 196–200. Mainline or "liberal" churches are just as susceptible to such influence.

³³Cf., Gibson Winter, *Liberating Creation: Foundations of a Religious Social Ethics* (New York: Crossroad, 1981), 75–80, and Anderson, *Walking the Way*, 258–59. Cf., Wink, *Engaging the Powers*, 300–301.

³⁴Alternative voices surfaced, such as in the debate by Martin L. Cook, Glen Stassen, Jean Bethke Elshtain, and James Turner Johnson in "Terrorism and 'Just War,'" *The Christian Century*, 14 November 2001, 22–29, and William Vance Trollinger Jr., "Nonviolent Voices: Peace Churches Make a Witness," *The Christian Century* (December 12, 2001): 18–22.

³⁵Among the most cogent analyses of 9/11 and the shift in U.S. policy on war, see a series of review articles in *The New York Review of Books*: Thomas Powers, "Secrets of September 11," 10 October 2002, 47–52; Felix Rohatyn, "From New York to Baghdad," 21 November 2002, 4–6; Joan Didion, "Fixed Options or the Hinge of History?" 16 January 2003, 54–59; Ronald Dworkin, "Terror and the Attack on Civil Liberties," 6 November 2003, 37–41.

³⁶Mark Horst, "Preaching from Ground Zero," *The Christian Century* (September 11, 2002): 40–43.

³⁷Walter Brueggemann, *Finally Comes the Poet: Daring Speech for Proclamation* (Minneapolis: Fortress Press, 1989), 68.

³⁸Walter Brueggemann, *Israel's Praise: Doxology against Idolatry and Ideology* (Philadelphia: Fortress Press, 1988), 128 and 12.

³⁹Walter Brueggemann, "Off by Nine Miles," *The Christian Century* 19–26 December 2001: 15.

⁴⁰Charles L. Campbell, foreword to *The Threat of Life: Sermons on Pain, Power, and Weakness*, by Walter Brueggemann, ed. Charles L. Campbell (Minneapolis: Fortress Press, 1996), ix. When Paul Wilson grapples with ethics and scripture in *God Sense: Reading the Bible for Preaching* (Nashville: Abingdon Press, 2001), he rightly stresses the importance of raising the questions, "Who is God? What is God saying? What is God doing?" (p. 67), and in chapter 7, "The Moral Sense."

⁴¹Martin Luther King Jr., "Beyond Vietnam," republished in "A Prophecy for the '80s," *Sojourners* 12, no. 1 (January 1983): 10–16, also available online at http:/

www.stanford.edu/group/King//publications/. On King's preaching, see also Richard Lischer, "King, Martin Luther, Jr.," *Concise Encyclopedia of Preaching,* ed. William H. Willimon and Richard Lischer (Louisville, Ky.: Westminster John Knox Press, 1995), 288-90. It should be noted that African American and predominately Caucasian congregations differ from each other in that the former give far more permission to preachers to speak about political issues than do most of the latter.

[42]King, "Beyond Vietnam."

[43]This is made abundantly clear by Vince Harding, "The Land Beyond: Reflections on King's Speech," *Sojourners* 12, no. 1 (January 1983): 18-22. Harding links this sermon directly with King's assassination.

[44]The ideological power of "free-market economics" is similarly overwhelming today. Middleton and Walsh call this "an ideological form of genocide," in *Truth Is Stranger Than It Used to Be,* 72.

[45]Nora Tubbs Tisdale is dealing with the command of Jesus that we love our enemies, "The Gospel We Don't Want to Hear (or Preach)," *Journal for Preachers* 23, no. 3 (Easter 2000): 23-30.

[46]Brueggemann, *Finally Comes the Poet,* 109-10. See in the final chapter the discussion of what James Kay calls preaching with a "bifocal vision."

Chapter 6: Authority

[1]Terry Anderson, *Walking the Way: Christian Ethics as a Guide* (Toronto: United Church Publishing House, 1993), 215-16.

[2]See J. Philip Wogaman, *Christian Ethics: A Historical Introduction* (Louisville, Ky.: Westminster John Knox Press, 1993), 278; and Anderson, *Walking the Way,* 216-32. For a critique that challenges particularly hegemonic appeals to the Bible, theology, experience, and culture, see John S. McClure, *Other-wise Preaching: A Postmodern Ethic for Homiletics* (St. Louis: Chalice Press, 2002).

[3]The example of differences over the use of inclusive language comes to mind.

[4]This question will be explored in the next chapter on the preacher's authority.

[5]Appeals to experience in scripture are not without difficulty. Joseph in Egypt looks back at his life and declares to his brothers, "God sent me before you to preserve for you a remnant on earth" (Gen. 45:7). How does a sense of God's providence correlate with Joseph's actions when these later result in a massive enslavement of his people in Egypt to Pharaoh (47:25-26)? Is Joseph's perspective of God's leading in his life in the short term open to challenge when his policies have enslaving effects as time goes on? See M. Douglas Meeks, *God the Economist: The Doctrine of God and Political Economy* (Minneapolis: Fortress Press, 1989), 78-80. Yet it is possible to say that even when we may claim God's providence inappropriately, God's ways constantly transcend our failures—as in the eventual exodus from Egypt.

[6]Fred B. Craddock, "My Mother's Name Is Grace," a taped sermon preached at Yorkminster Park Baptist Church, Toronto, August 14, 1994.

[7]At this point Craddock comments on how similar this description is to that of Paul's experiences in such passages as 1 Cor. 2:3-4; 1 Thess. 2:7, 11, 17; and Rom. 16:13.

[8]Michael Welker, *God the Spirit* (Minneapolis: Fortress Press, 1994), 46-47.

[9]Chopp, *Saving Work: Feminist Practices of Theological Education* (Louisville, Ky.: Westminster John Knox Press, 1995), 61, 66.

[10]In chapter 5 I referred to a reflection piece by Nora Tubbs Tisdale about forgiving one's enemies, one that I subsequently heard her preach in revised form. Her appeal to her own experience in the aftermath of the terrorist attacks (of September 2001) enabled me to hear this word of gospel more deeply and convincingly.

[11]Lisa Sowle Cahill, "Using Empirical Information," in *From Christ to the World: Introductory Reading in Christian Ethics,* ed. Wayne G. Boulton, Thomas D. Kennedy,

and Allen Verhey (Grand Rapids, Mich.: Eerdmans, 1994), 177–79, an excerpt from her *Between the Sexes* (Philadelphia: Fortress Press; New York: Paulist Press, 1985).

[12] James M. Gustafson, "The Relation of Empirical Science to Moral Thought," in *From Christ to the World*, 164–65, an excerpt from *Proceeding of the Catholic Theological Society of America* 26 (1971): 122–37.

[13] Anderson, *Walking the Way*, 218. While there are notable exceptions (such as Max Stackhouse), Protestant thinkers have tended toward the former and Roman Catholics to the latter.

[14] Max L. Stackhouse, *Apologia: Contextualization, Globalization, and Mission in Theological Education* (Grand Rapids, Mich.: Eerdmans, 1988), 210–14; and "The Vocation of Christian Ethics Today," *The Princeton Seminary Bulletin* 16, no. 3 (1995): 302.

[15] This may be part of the reason why David Tracy speaks of people having both a natural hermeneutical competence and a natural religious competence: *Plurality and Ambiguity: Hermeneutics, Religion, Hope* (San Francisco: Harper & Row, 1989), 103. This also seems implied in the sermon discussions shared by the whole congregation in the Christian Base Community of Solentiname, Nicaragua. See Ernesto Cardinal, *The Gospel in Solentiname* (Maryknoll, N.Y.: Orbis Books, 1982), vols. 1–4.

[16] Nancy Murphy and George F. R. Ellis, *On the Moral Nature of the Universe: Theology, Cosmology, and Ethics* (Minneapolis: Fortress Press, 1996), 194–96. Their term *kenotic* is based on the self-emptying of Jesus referred to in Phil. 2:7. Cf., Lesslie Newbigin, *Foolishness to the Greeks: The Gospel and Western Culture* (London: SPCK, 1986), 102–6; and John B. Cobb Jr., "Faith Seeking Understanding: The Renewal of Christian Thinking," *The Christian Century* (June 29, 1994): 642–44.

[17] John Habgood, *Being a Person: Where Faith and Science Meet* (London: Hodder & Stoughton, 1998), 280–81.

[18] Preaching is always contextual. A congregation with primarily one assumption would be addressed in another way.

[19] See Gabriel Fackre, "Preaching about Abortion," in *Restoring the Center: Essays Evangelical and Ecumenical* (Downers Grove, Ill.: InterVarsity Press, 1998), 144–48.

[20] Newbigin, *Foolishness to the Greeks*, 52–64; see also Don Wardlaw, "Preaching as the Interface of Two Social Worlds" in *Preaching as a Social Act: Theology and Practice*, ed. Arthur Van Seters (Nashville: Abingdon Press, 1988), 55–84.

[21] Brueggemann, *Theology of the Old Testament: Testimony, Dispute, Advocacy* (Minneapolis: Fortress Press, 1997), 578–87, 604–10. A central organizing principle in Brueggemann's lengthy volume reveals the intricacy and variety of Israel's traditions through a kind of courtroom drama in which testimony is given, countered, and added to with unsolicited voices (including the nations and creation), and finally mediated through the testimony of Torah, king, prophet, cult, and sage.

[22] Wogaman, *Christian Ethics*, 270.

[23] Ibid., 276.

[24] Alasdair MacIntyre, *After Virtue: A Study in Moral Theory*, 2d ed. (Notre Dame, Ind.: University of Notre Dame Press, 1984), 220–24. MacIntyre deals at length with the nature and choice of traditions and their concomitant rationalities in *Whose Justice? Which Rationality?* (Notre Dame, Ind.: University of Notre Dame Press, 1988), see especially the final chapter. MacIntyre's views are discussed by J. Richard Middleton and Brian J. Walsh, *Truth Is Stranger Than It Used to Be: Biblical Faith in a Postmodern Age* (Downers Grove, Ill.: Inter-Varsity Press, 1995), 66–68; and Nancey Murphy and George F. R. Ellis, *On the Moral Nature of the Universe* (Minneapolis: Fortress Press: 1996), 13–15, 115–116, 221–223.

[25] Walter Wink, *Engaging the Powers: Discernment and Resistance in a World of Domination* (Minneapolis: Fortress Press, 1992), 13–49. Cf., Stanley Hauerwas and Charles Pinches, *Christians Among the Virtues: Theological Conversations with Ancient and Modern Ethics* (Notre Dame, Ind.: University of Notre Dame Press, 1997), 61–119.

[26] M. Shawn Copeland, "The Wounds of Jesus, The Wounds of My People," *Telling the Truth: Preaching about Sexual and Domestic Violence,* ed. John S. McClure and Nancy J. Ramsay (Cleveland: United Church Press, 1998), 39.

[27] Copeland offers excellent sermons on domestic violence, with specific articles on homiletics as well (ibid., 40–45). Cf., Ted Peters, *Sin: Radical Evil in Soul and Society* (Grand Rapids, Mich.: Eerdmans, 1994), chap. 5.

[28] Lisa Sowle Cahill, "Sexual Ethics: A Feminist Biblical Perspective," *Interpretation* 49, no. 1 (January 1995): 5–16, offers an approach to tradition that seeks to understand the kind of New Testament Christian community that she believes could help the church today in its debates regarding homosexuality. This contrasts with other appeals to tradition that emphasize the church's 2,000 years of viewing homosexual acts as morally wrong.

[29] I am drawing here on Walter Brueggemann's recent and highly accessible summary, "Biblical Authority: A Personal Reflection," *The Christian Century* (January 3, 2001): 14–20.

[30] Here, I am indebted to Sandra M. Schneiders, "Scripture as Word of God," *The Princeton Seminary Bulletin* 14, no. 1 (1993): 18–35.

[31] Andrew T. Lincoln, "Gospel Truth in the Fourth Gospel?" (paper presented at Wycliffe College, Toronto, October 21, 1998). Cf., Paul Ricoeur, "The Hermeneutics of Testimony," in *Essays on Biblical Interpretation,* ed. Lewis S. Mudge (Philadelphia: Fortress Press, 1980), 119–54.

[32] Richard B. Hays, *The Moral Vision of the New Testament, Community, Cross, New Creation: A Contemporary Introduction to New Testament Ethics* (New York: HarperCollins, 1996), 3–7, 379–406. I offer a highly simplified version of Hays' approach. Along the way I refer to and note some other points of view. My purpose is not to settle this issue but to clarify what is involved in appealing to scripture.

[33] William H. Willimon, "Postmodern Preaching: Learning to Love the Thickness of the Text," *Journal for Preachers* 19, no. 3 (Easter 1996): 33–34.

[34] Sarah J. Molcher, "The Holiness Code and Human Sexuality," in *Biblical Ethics and Homosexuality,* ed. Robert L. Brawley (Louisville, Ky.: Westminster John Knox Press, 1996), 87–102.

[35] Martin S. Cohen, "The Biblical Prohibition of Homosexuality," an unpublished paper presented at the Vancouver School of Theology, 1990.

[36] Hays, *Moral Vision,* 388–89.

[37] Ulrich Mauser, "Creation and Human Sexuality," in *Biblical Ethics and Homosexuality: Listening to Scripture,* ed. Robert L. Brawley (Louisville, Ky.: Westminster John Knox Press, 1996), 3–15. Feminists point out that this paradigm sets up a hierarchy in which heterosexual people are more complete, and persons who are single or homosexual are incomplete. See the discussion in the next section.

[38] Mary McClintock Fulkerson, "Church Documents on Human Sexuality and the Authority of Scripture," *Interpretation* 49, no. 1 (January 1995): 53–54. Fulkerson includes in this trajectory the exodus, the prophetic emphasis on justice, the centrality of love in the ministry of Jesus, and the welcoming nature of the early church.

[39] In selecting these three, Hays is consciously not including love or liberation as great New Testament imperatives. In this he moves against many others who appeal to both. See *Moral Vision,* 200–203.

[40] See, for example, Robin Scroggs, "The Bible as Foundation Document," *Interpretation* 49, no. 1 (January 1995): 17–30.

[41] In my paper *Seeing beyond the Horizon,* Occasional Paper, 4 (published by the Vancouver School of Theology), 14, I have explored Paul Ricoeur's notion of *appropriation* as a daring step of faith when the interpreter enters "the world in front of the text" (Ricoeur's language) imaginatively in a process of *letting go* so that its revelatory power effects in us a new ability to believe. Cf., Ricoeur, *The Symbolism of Evil,* trans. Emerson Buchanan (New York: Harper & Row, 1967), 350–53; *Hermeneutics and the Human Sciences: Essays on Language, Action, and Interpretation,* ed. and trans. John B. Thompson (Cambridge, England: Cambridge University Press, 1981), 189–91; and

Essays on Biblical Interpretation, ed. Lewis S. Mudge (Philadelphia: Fortress Press, 1980), 15, 119–54.

[42]Middleton and Walsh, *Truth Is Stranger,* 175. Hays uses the analogy of music to describe this as "constructive improvisation," *Moral Vision,* 6. For another alternative, see Cahill, "Sexual Ethics," 5, 8. She reads the text not as norm-oriented but in terms of its description of a resocialized community and asks what kind of community should the church be today with regard to homosexual persons.

[43]Mary Stewart Van Leeuwen, "To Ask a Better Question: The Heterosexuality–Homosexuality Debate Revisited," *Interpretation* 51, no. 2 (April 1997): 150–56.

[44]Walter Brueggemann, *Interpretation and Obedience: From Faithful Reading to Faithful Living* (Minneapolis: Fortress Press, 1991), 1.

[45]Earlier I noted that in this section we were not seeking to decide the right or wrong response to a given moral question but how our exploration of each question involves the way we appeal to various authorities.

[46]For opposing views, see Fulkerson, "Church Documents," and Van Leeuwen, "To Ask a Better Question."

[47]See Letty M. Russell, "Authority and the Challenge of Feminist Interpretation," in *Feminist Interpretation of the Bible,* ed. Letty Russell (Philadelphia: Westminster Press, 1985), 145–46. Russell refers specifically to the position of Elisabeth Schüssler Fiorenza as over against her own.

[48]Anderson, *Walking the Way,* 226, 230.

[49]Lisa Sowle Cahill, "Moral Methodology: A Case Study," in *Introduction to Christian Ethics,* ed. Ronald P. Hamel and Kenneth R. Hines (Mahwah, N.J.: Paulist Press, 1989), 562. This case study focuses specifically on the issue of homosexuality.

Chapter 7: Preacher, Sermon, and Congregation

[1]Fred B. Craddock, *Preaching* (Nashville: Abingdon Press, 1985), 51–52.

[2]William H. Willimon, "Be Imitators of Me," in *Preaching to Strangers* (Louisville, Ky.: Westminster/John Knox Press, 1992), 47.

[3]I am not implying that such materials could not be useful when used appropriately. This also means that we should not represent other people's work as though it were our own.

[4]Will D. Campbell, *Brother to a Dragonfly* (New York: Continuum, 1997), 182.

[5]See J. Philip Wogaman's chapter, "The Pastoral and the Prophetic," in *Speaking the Truth in Love: Prophetic Preaching to a Broken World* (Louisville, Ky.: Westminster John Knox Press, 1998), 18–27.

[6]Joseph A. Edelheit, "An Ethics for the Interpretation of Contemporary Jewish Experience," in *Clergy Ethics in a Changing Society: Mapping the Terrain,* ed. James P. Wind et al. (Louisville, Ky.: Westminster/John Knox Press, 1991), 257–58. Edelheit contrasts knowledge with understanding. Knowledge requires disciplined, objective study and should be as definite as possible. Understanding acknowledges human subjectivity and limitations and therefore entails the willingness to remain open to more learning. These two need to be held in tension with each other in moral reasoning. See also David Tracy's discussion of interpretation as conversation that fails if it demands certitude, *Plurality and Ambiguity: Hermeneutics, Religion, Hope* (San Francisco: Harper & Row, 1989), 22–23.

[7]Charles Campbell, *The Word Before the Powers: An Ethic of Preaching* (Louisville, Ky.: Westminster John Knox Press, 2002), 157.

[8]I have tried to demonstrate this in my sermon in the appendix.

[9]Martin E. Marty speaks of these norms as once theologically and ecclesiastically sanctioned, "Clergy Ethics in America: The Ministers on Their Own," in *Clergy Ethics,* 23–29.

[10]Christopher Lasch, *The Culture of Narcissism: American Life in an Age of Diminished Expectations* (New York: W. W. Norton, 1979), 12, 181.

11. Fred B. Craddock, *As One Without Authority*, 3d ed. (Nashville: Abingdon Press, 1979), 11, 14.

12. Ibid., 128-29.

13. Christine Smith, *Weaving the Sermon: Preaching in a Feminist Perspective* (Louisville, Ky.: Westminster/John Knox Press, 1989), 48-49, 51-52. See also Leonora Tubbs Tisdale, "Women's Ways of Communicating: A New Blessing for Preaching," in *Women, Gender, and Christian Community*, ed. Jane Dempsey Douglass and James F. Kay (Louisville: Westminster John Knox Press, 1997). Other liberationist perspectives— reflecting race or class, for example—also share an emphasis on the authority of experience. It should be added that the issue of inclusive language is a moral one. Language that hides, stereotypes, or diminishes others undermines a gospel based on grace.

14. Robert S. Reid, "Postmodernism and the Function of the New Homiletic in Post-Christendom Congregations," *Homiletic* 22, no. 2 (Winter 1995): 7-11. The evolution of homiletic form has been described in some detail by Thomas G. Long, with an interesting closing comment that the sermon may have to return to a reemphasis on knowledge because listeners are increasingly unaware of the basic content of the faith. "Form," in *Concise Encyclopedia of Preaching*, ed. William H. Willimon and Richard Lischer (Louisville: Westminster John Knox Press, 1995), 144-51.

15. David M. Greenhaw, "As One *With* Authority," in *Intersections: Post-Critical Studies in Preaching*, ed. Richard L. Eslinger (Grand Rapids, Mich.: Eerdmans, 1994), 105, 119-21. Sermons must be more than storytelling, just as they must also be more than concepts (pp. 112-13). William Willimon is far more critical than Greenhaw of Craddock's position on the preacher's authority. He sees it as a capitulation to modernity's notion of individualistic freedom in which method and style are more important than message and substance. To be fair, Willimon acknowledges that in later writings Craddock puts more emphasis on the place of scripture in preaching. Willimon, *Peculiar Speech: Preaching to the Baptized* (Grand Rapids, Mich.: Eerdmans, 1992), 47-53.

16. Thomas G. Long, *The Witness of Preaching* (Louisville, Ky.: Westminster/John Knox Press, 1989), 44. See also Paul Ricoeur, "The Hermeneutics of Testimony," in *Essays on Biblical Interpretation*, ed. Lewis S. Mudge (Philadelphia: Fortress Press, 1980), 119-54; and Arthur Van Seters, "Preaching Justice: The Witness of the Spirit," *Papers of the Annual Meeting of the Academy of Homiletics* (Toronto, December 7-10, 1983): 41-47.

17. M. L. Brownsberger, "Ethos, Incarnation and Responsibility," in *Clergy Ethics*, 152.

18. Campbell, *Word Before the Powers*, 81.

19. See R. S. Sugirtharajah, "'For You Always Have the Poor with You': An Example of Hermeneutics of Suspicion," *The Asian Journal of Theology* 4, no. 1 (April 1990): 102-7.

20. See especially, David Buttrick, "Afterword: Looking toward a Future," *A Captive Voice: The Liberation of Preaching* (Louisville, Ky.: Westminster/John Knox Press, 1994), 100-113. Cf., Wogaman, *Speaking the Truth in Love*, 41-43.

21. I am thinking here of Christine Smith, Joseph A. Edelheit, and David Tracy, all referred to earlier in this chapter.

22. See John Habgood, "Knowing Good and Evil," in *Being a Person: Where Faith and Science Meet* (London: Hodder & Stoughton, 1998), 257-81.

23. See the introductory notes and accompanying sermons in the chapters on the topical sermon, preaching on a biblical theme, or social issues in Ronald Allen, ed., *Patterns of Preaching: A Sermon Sampler* (St. Louis, Mo.: Chalice Press, 1998), 149-70, 199-206.

24. For a different reading of this parable see William R. Herzog II, *Parables as Subversive Speech: Jesus as Pedagogue of the Oppressed* (Louisville, Ky.: Westminster John Knox Press, 1994), 150-68.

[25] Don S. Browning, *Religious Ethics and Pastoral Care* (Philadelphia: Fortress Press, 1983), 53, 120-21. Cf., Anderson, "The Art of Discerning the Way," in *Walking the Way*, 241-74.

[26] Moral reflection, for Anderson, includes some moral tradition, an ethical framework, a common moral language, deliberative forums, appropriate processes, a style of discourse, and the gifts of the Spirit in the church; *Walking the Way*, 269-72.

[27] "The Crooked E: The Unshredded Truth about Enron," CTV, January 5, 2003.

[28] See Miroslav Volf, *Exclusion and Embrace: A Theological Exploration of Identity, Otherness, and Reconciliation* (Nashville: Abingdon Press, 1996), 125-31.

[29] James F. Kay, "The Word of the Cross at the Turn of the Ages," *Interpretation* 53, no. 1 (January 1999): 51.

[30] Cf., Walter Johnson, "The Ethics of Preaching," *Interpretation* 20, no. 4 (October 1966): 412-31.

[31] Rebecca Chopp, "Liberating Ministry," in *Clergy Ethics*, 87, 94-95.

[32] Michael Welker, *God the Spirit* (Minneapolis: Fortress Press, 1994), 234, 239-40.

[33] Chopp, "Liberating Ministry," 93. Chopp contrasts the *constitutive community* with one that is *instrumental* (where individuals only agree "to cooperate to meet their own needs") or one that is *sentimental* (people associate because of motivations shared just among themselves).

[34] Walter Brueggemann, *Finally Comes the Poet: Daring Speech for Proclamation* (Minneapolis: Fortress Press, 1989), 137. Bringing their lives to the Word is one of the stellar contributions of participatory preaching in the Christian Base Communities of Latin America. See especially Carlos Mesters, "The Use of the Bible in Christian Communities of the Common People," in *The Challenge of Basic Christian Communities,* ed. Sergio Torres and John Eagleson (Maryknoll, N.Y.: Orbis Books, 1981), 197-210.

[35] Brownsberger, "Ethos, Incarnation and Responsibility," 141, 153.

[36] See the chapter, "Interpretation: The Listeners," in Craddock, *Preaching,* 84-98.

[37] Stanley Hauerwas in *Preaching to Strangers* (Louisville, Ky.: Westminster/John Knox Press, 1992), 53.

[38] J. Richard Middleton and Brian J. Walsh, *Truth Is Stranger Than It Used to Be: Biblical Faith in a Postmodern Age* (Downers Grove, Ill.: InterVarsity Press, 1995), 175, 181-83. Cf., Don Wardlaw, "Preaching as the Interface of Two Social Worlds," in *Preaching as a Social Act: Theology and Practice,* ed. Arthur Van Seters (Nashville: Abingdon Press, 1988), 55-93.

[39] In spring 2001, I was part of an ecumenical mission to Sudan. While in Nairobi, Kenya, our group spoke with Timothy Njoya, who shared these remarks with us. Richard Bauckham notes this eschatological perspective in Moltmann's view of the church. See his "Jürgen Moltmann," *The Modern Theologians: An Introduction to Christian Theology,* vol. 1, ed. David F. Ford (Oxford: Blackwell, 1989), 293-301.

Author Index

A
Abby, Deb, 150
Allen, Ronald J., 152, 158
Anderson, Terence R., ix–x, 33, 52, 141, 142, 143, 144, 145, 147, 148, 149, 150, 151, 154, 155, 157, 158, 159
Aquinas, Thomas, 46
Aristotle, 46, 48
Augustine, 6–7, 142
Austen, Jane, 10

B
Baker, David, 152
Barr, Robert R., 152
Bauckham, Richard, 159
Baum, Gregory, 151
Berger, Peter L., 142
Bernardo, Paul, 45
Blair, Tony, 145
Blatchford, Christie, 146
Bobo, Kim, 151
Boesak, Allan, 153
Bonhoeffer, Dietrich, 44, 79, 151
Boulton, Wayne G., 142, 144, 150, 151, 154
Bragg, Rebecca, 148
Brawley, Robert L., 156
Brill-Edwards, Michelle, 56–57, 145
Brooks, Leonard J., 148
Browning, Don S., 127, 159
Brownsberger, M. L., 131, 158, 159
Brueggemann, Walter, 18, 93–94, 143, 145, 149, 153, 154, 155, 156, 157, 159
Buckman, Robert, 9–10, 142

Bush, George W., 93, 148
Butler, Joseph, 7
Buttrick, David, 10, 126, 142, 158

C
Cahill, Lisa Sowle, 103, 143, 149, 154, 155, 156, 157
Calvin, John, 6, 148–49
Campbell, Charles L., viii, 14, 33, 94, 139, 143, 144, 145, 146, 152, 153, 157–58
Campbell, Will D., 62, 122, 148, 157
Cardinal, Ernesto, 155
Carl, William J., III, 149
Carter, Stephen, 44, 146, 150
Cassidy, John, 34, 141, 144, 145, 148
Chappell, Tom, 75, 149, 150
Charry, Ellen, 148, 149
Chopp, Rebecca, 91, 102, 130, 143, 152, 153, 154, 159
Cibelli, Jose B., 145
Clinton, Bill, 145
Cobb, John B., Jr., 151, 155
Cochrane, Charles A., 6, 141
Coffin, William Sloane, 77, 151
Cohen, Martin S., 156
Collins, Chuck. 75
Conyers, A. J., 144
Cook, Martin L., 153
Cooper, Austin, 45–46, 146
Copeland, M. Shawn, 109–10, 156
Cousar, Charles B., 147, 148
Craddock, Fred, 17, 67, 101–2, 120, 123–24, 154, 157, 158, 159

Crossman, Richard, 32, 145

D
Dalferth, Ingolf U., 144
Daniel, Eileen L, 141
Davis, Miles, 148
Della Fave, Richard, 151
Didion, Joan, 141, 153
Douglass, Jane Dempsey, 153, 158
Dudley, Carl S., 88, 152
Dutcher-Walls, Patricia, 149
Dworkin, Ronald, 153

E
Eagleson, John, 159
Edelheit, Joseph A., 157, 158
Edwards, Jonathan, 7
Ehnes, Herbert, 145
Eliot, T. S., 2
Elliott, Charles, 81, 151
Ellis, George F. R., 104, 155
Elshtain, Jean Bethke, 153
Eslinger, Richard L., 158
Evans, Bill, 61, 148
Ezzell, Carol, 145

F
Fackre, Gabriel, 155
Farley, Wendy, 37–39, 146
Farnsley, Arthur E., II, 152
Finn, Daniel Rush, 150
Fiorenza, Elisabeth Schüssler, 157
Ford, David F., 159
Fortune, Marie, 37–38, 146
Freire, Paulo, 91, 122, 153
Fulkerson, Mary McClintock, 156
Furnish, Victor Paul, 142

G
Gerrish, Brian, 56, 148
Gewirth, Alan, 151
Glaz, Maxine, 146
Goar, Carol, 150

Graham, Gordon, 150, 88, 152
Gravely, Patrick, 45
Greenhaw, David M., 124, 158
Grenz, Stanley J., 145, 152
Grindal, Gracia, 57–58, 148
Gula, Richard M., 149
Gustafson, James M., 103, 155

H
Habgood, John, 105, 145, 155, 158
Hall, Douglas John, 145
Hamel, Ronald P., 143, 157
Handel, George Frederick, 25
Harding, Vince, 154
Harrison, Beverly W., 143
Hauerwas, Stanley, 19, 48–50, 132, 142, 143, 144, 147, 148, 149, 153, 155, 159
Hays, Richard B., 113–14, 141, 156, 157
Heim, David, 142
Herman, Stewart, 150
Herzog II, William R., 144, 158
Hessel, Dieter T., 148
Hines, Kenneth R., 143, 157
Holmgren, Stephen, 143
Homolka, Karla, 45
Horst, Mark, 93, 153
Hospers, John, 152
Hough, Joseph C., Jr., 143
Hume, David, 142

I
Ignatieff, Michael, 142, 151
Ignatius of Antioch, 6

J
Johnson, James Turner, 153
Johnson, Lyndon, 94
Johnson, W. Walter, 143, 159
Jones, L. Gregory, 149

K
Kant, Immanuel, 47
Kasmeirski, Mary Ann, 73

Kay, James F., 129, 140, 153, 158–59
Kennedy, John F., 95
Kennedy, Thomas D., 142, 143, 144, 150, 151, 154
Kierkegaard, Søren, 7, 142
Kim, Ken, 15, 143
King, Martin Luther, Jr., 16, 94–95, 153, 154
Kogawa, Joy, 76, 151
Krieg, Carmen, 144
Kucharz, Thomas, 144

L

Laidlaw, Stuart, 145
Lakey, Jack, 144
Lanza, Robert P., 145
Lasch, Christopher, 123, 157
Latimer, Laura, Robert and Tracy, 68–71, 73
Lawal, Amina, 136, 139
Lebacqz, Karen, 150
Leishman, Rory, 151
Lewis, Anthony, 148
Lincoln, Andrew T., 156
Lischer, Richard, 143, 148, 149, 151, 154, 158
Lochhead, David, 142
Locke, John, 47
Long, Thomas G., 124–25, 141, 143, 158
Lovin, Robert, 142
Lukwiya, Matthew, 16
Luther, Martin, 6

M

MacCharles, Tonda, 150
MacIntyre, Alasdair, 4, 10, 108, 141, 142, 144, 147, 150, 155
Maduro, Otto, 152
Maguire, Daniel, 142
Mandela, Nelson, 53, 147
Marty, Martin E., 123, 142, 157
Mauser, Ulrich, 156

Mayer, Jane, 148
Mays, James Luther, 145, 147
McAteer, Michael, 142
McCann, J. Clinton, Jr., 149, 150
McClure, John S., 38, 146, 152, 154, 156
McKenzie, Alyce M., 55, 147
McQuaig, Linda, 144
Meador, Keith G., 149
Meeks, M. Douglas, 141, 154
Meilaender, Gilbert, 150
Mesters, Carlos, 159
Middleton, J. Richard, 152, 154, 155, 157, 159
Moessner, Jeanne Stevenson, 146
Molcher, Sarah J., 156
Moltmann, Jürgen, 25, 144, 145, 159
Moyers, Bill, 70, 149
Mudge, Lewis S., 141, 144, 156, 157
Murphy, Nancy, 104, 155
Murray, Ken, 45, 50, 146

N

Newbigin, Lesslie, 76, 88, 151, 155
Niebuhr, Reinhold, 7, 11, 50, 64, 142, 147, 148, 149
Njoya, Timothy, 159
Noll, Mark A., 23, 144, 153
Nozick, Robert, 151

O

Ogletree, Thomas W., 141
Olive, David, 148
Origen, 6

P

Papp, Lester, 141
Paton, Alan, 76, 151
Patte, Daniel, 144
Pellegrino, Edward, 46–48, 50, 146, 147

Peters, John, 150
Peters, Ted, 57, 145, 148, 149, 156
Philips, Derek, 150, 151
Phillips, David, 27, 144
Phuc, Kim, 56
Pinches, Charles, 155
Potok, Chaim, 147, 150
Powers, Thomas, 153
Preston, Richard, 145
Priestley, J. B., 56

R

Ramsay, Nancy J., 146, 156
Rawls, John, 151
Reid, Robert S., 158
Ricoeur, Paul, 141, 156, 158
Rieger, Jeorg, 151
Rifkin, Jeremy, 3, 141
Rohatyn, Felix, 153
Romero, Oscar, 56
Russell, Letty M., 157
Rutledge, Fleming, 66, 149

S

Saul, John Ralston, 152
Schaffer, Arthur, 69–70, 149
Schiller, Bill, 141,
Schleiermacher, Friedrich, 7
Schneiders, Sandra M., 156
Scroggs, Robin, 156
Sherman, Amy L., 152
Sider, Ronald F., 81, 151
Smith, Christine, 158
Smith, J. Alfred, 148
Sobrino, Jon, 92, 153
Socrates, 11
Somerville, Margaret, 145, 149
Spencer, Herbert, 152
Stackhouse, Max, 104, 155
Stassen, Glen, 153
Stefaniuk, Walter, 144
Stringfellow, William, viii, 89, 152

Sugirtharajah, R. S., 158

T

Talaga, Tanya, 141
Taylor, Barbara Brown, 14, 143
Tertullian, 6
Theoharis, Liz, 151
Thomas, J. Mark, 152
Tisdale, Nora Tubbs, 95, 153, 154, 158
Toffler, Barbara Ley, 50, 145, 147
Toobin, Jeffrey, 148
Torres, Sergio, 159
Towler, Robert, 142
Townes, Emilie, 142
Tracy, David, 155, 157, 158
Trible, Phyllis, 91, 152
Trollinger, William Vance, Jr., 153

U

Unruh, Heidi Rolland, 152

V

Van Leeuwen, Mary Stewart, 157
Van Seters, Arthur, 141, 143, 145, 155, 156, 158, 159
Vanier, Jean, 56, 71, 150
Verhey, Allen, 142, 144, 149, 151, 155
Vineberg, Phyllis, 144
Visser, Margaret, 150
Volf, Miroslav, 22–23, 72, 143, 144, 147, 150, 159
Von Waldow, H. Eberhard, 152

W

Walsh, Brian J., 152, 154, 155, 157, 159
Wardlaw, Don M., 141, 143, 155, 159
Welker, Michael, 102, 129, 144, 154, 159
Wesley, John and Charles, 7

West, Michael, 145
Wheeler, Barbara G., 143
Whitefield, George, 7
Wiesel, Elie, 11, 25, 142
Willimon, William H., 51–52,
    67, 113, 132, 143, 147, 149,
    156, 157, 158
Wilson, Paul Scott, x, 153
Wind, James P., 142, 157
Wink, Walter, 92, 147, 153, 155,
Winter, Gibson, 153
Wogaman, Philip, 5–6, 35,
    107–8, 141, 143, 146,
    154, 155, 157, 158

Y

Young, Alan, 46, 146

Scripture Index

Genesis
1	74
1 and 2	106, 114
1:26–27	17
1:26–28	29
3	126
45:7	154
47	8
47:13–26	4
47:25–26	154

Exodus
19	107
19–20	64
20	110
20:1–7	65
20:8–17	65
21:22–23	17, 106
22:21–27	72
24	64

Leviticus
18:22	114
25	16

Deuteronomy
5:6–11	65
5:12–21	65
6:5	65
7:7–9	5
15	5, 8
15:11	126

Judges
4:1	72
5:11	72

Ruth
book of	5

2 Samuel
7	107

1 Kings
3:14	107
9:4–8	107

Nehemiah
5	88

Psalms
8	29
8:4–5	29
19:1–3	100
24:1	9
89	107
119:105	4
132	107

Proverbs
31:8–9	35

Isaiah
53	151
58	88
60	94

Jeremiah
1:4–5	17
31:33	107

Ezekiel
36:26–27	107

Amos
3:2	5

Jonah
book of	5

Micah
2	94
6:8	62, 73

Zechariah
8:4–5	35

Sirach
35:15a, 16b–17, 21a	136

Matthew
1:18–23	17
5–7	66–67, 110
5:31–32	5
5:48	67
6:28–33	28
7:43–48	149
11:4	100
11:5	88
25	88
25:14–30	126–27
26:11	125

Mark
6:5–6	130
7:21–22	147
12:29–31	68
12:30	65, 104

Luke
1:52	137
9:23	63
10	72
18:1–8	135–39
24	51

John
4:24	112
7:17	113
11:50	151
13:34	63, 95
15:12, 17	95

Acts
17:22–31	5

Romans
1:18–32	114
1:29–31	147
2:1	114
4:5	73
5:21	34
6:17	34
8	35, 93
9–11	5
12:2	52, 92, 104
12:6–8	147
12:10	95
13:8	95
13	viii
16:13	154

1 Corinthians
2:2, 4	129
2:3–4	154
2:6–8	92
2:10, 16	129
2:16	45, 104
6:9–10	147
12	54
12:7–11	147

2 Corinthians
3:2–3	132
4:5	121
5:17	15
12:20	147

Galatians
2:20	15, 121
5	53, 110
5:1	48
5:16	57
6:2	63

Ephesians
1:16–23	30

Philippians
2:1–5	54
2:7	155
3:17	121

Colossians
1:15–16   34
1:22   34

1 Thessalonians
2:7, 11, 17   154
2:13   130
4:9   95

Hebrews
8   107

James
1:17   74
2:14–17   5

1 Peter
1:22   95

2 Peter
1:5–8   147

1 John
1:1   101
3:11, 14, 23   95
4:1   102
4:7, 11–12   95

2 John
1:5   95

Revelation
13   viii, 35
22   67

Subject Index

A
Anabaptists, 6
authority, 99–116
    church tradition, 107–10
    experience, 100–104, 124, 158
    interrelationship of, 115–16
    preacher's, 123–25
    reason, 104–7
    scripture, 106, 110–15, 125–26

C
church, 130–32
    conflicts, 24, 108
    empowered, 24–25, 102, 108, 130, 146, 159
    marginal, 24
    questions from history of, 6–8
culture (*see also* worldview), 2–4, 8, 16, 22–26, 30–31, 48–49, 53–55, 63, 71, 80, 90, 103, 108–9, 114, 121, 123–24, 147, 152, 157

E
ethical issues, 3–4
    abortion, 17, 105–6, 155
    domestic violence, 36–39, 109–10, 156
    genetics, human genome, 2–3, 31–33, 80, 90, 105–6, 115, 126, 141, 145
    justice, justice system, 23, 34, 39, 45–46, 68, 70–73, 88–89, 115, 135–39, 146, 147, 150, 152
    legalized gambling, 26–29, 115
    love of neighbor, 68–71
    market economics, business, corporate scandals, 34, 50, 55, 63, 74, 128, 131, 138, 147, 148, 150, 151, 152, 154
    mercy killing, 23, 68–71, 73, 149
    poverty, welfare and wealth, 16, 81, 85–89, 92, 115, 125–26, 152, 153
    professional behavior, 45–48, 50–51, 81–84, 89–91, 146, 147
    race, racism 16, 34–35, 94–95, 109, 151, 153, 154, 158
    September 11, 2001, x, 4, 22–23, 71, 93, 153, 154
    sexuality, gender, 36–39, 91–92, 100, 103, 109–10, 114–15, 124, 135–38, 153, 154, 156, 158
    war, security and peace, 23, 55, 80, 94–95, 138–39, 146, 148, 149, 151, 153
ethical reflection
    model, 12–17, 119–20, 142, 143
    centered in Christ, 9, 13–14, 23–24, 119, 125, 129, 140

ethics and
  deontology, 148
  freedom, 48–50, 66, 91, 129–30
  human rights and relationships, 75–77, 88, 152
  integrity, 43–45, 57–58
  obligation, 66, 149
  secularity, 9–12, 142, 145
  sin, wrath and forgiveness, 33–39, 53–54, 56–57, 146, 148
  utility, consequences, 47, 82, 149
  values, 73–75, 141

H
homiletics for ethics, 119–133
  assumptions, 14, 17–19, 100, 143, 158
  components, 143
  cross and Spirit-centered (*see also* ethical reflection model), 11–12, 18, 53–54, 58, 124–25, 129, 139–40
  guidelines, 28–29, 32–33, 39, 50–52, 55–58, 61, 84, 87, 89–90, 93, 95, 115–16, 149
  questions for preachers, 2–9, 18–19
  sermon examples, 35, 51–52, 56–58, 66, 81–84, 94–95, 101–2, 105–6, 135–39

M
moralism, moralizing, 53, 57, 139

P
pastoral and prophetic preaching, 77, 84, 94–95, 122, 133, 151, 152, 154

R
reason, wisdom, understanding, 34, 54, 147, 157
  and science, 25, 31–32, 51, 91, 106, 145

S
scripture
  interpretation, 111–15, 154, 155, 156, 157
  questions from, 4–5, 8
Sermon on the Mount, 5, 66–67, 108, 125, 148, 149
social analysis, 85–89
stories, illustrations, 84, 151
  A Few Good Men, 135
  Amina Lawal and Sharia, 136
  "An Inspector Calls," 56
  Bernardo trial, 45–46
  courage in El Salvador, 138–39
  conjoined twins and surgery, 81–84
  Craddock: "My Mother's Name Is Grace," 101–2
  dangerous worship, 52
  engaging a divisive issue, 1, 74
  getting theology for one's business, 75
  jazz improvisation, 61–62, 149
  no more tax breaks, 75
  operation to the cheek, 57–58
  Paulo Freire and service 121–22

Patch Adams and ideology, 90–91
saving Jews in World War II, 34–35
Wiesel: death of a boy in Nazi camp, 11, 142
winning at all costs, 44

T

Ten Commandments, 5, 64–68, 125, 149

W

World Alliance of Reformed Churches, 30–31
worldview, ideology, 21, 49, 80, 90–95, 143, 152, 153, 154

Printed in the United States
24827LVS00002B/79-408